The Drake Beam Morin Guide to Getting Started With Your Career

A Division of Drake Beam Morin, Inc.
100 Park Avenue, New York NY 10017
212 692-7700

Printed in the United States of America   ISBN: 1-880030-23-3

1   2   3   4   5   6   7   8   9

Table of contents

Charts, Indices and Demonstration Documents

Foreword

You have embarked on one of life's great adventures — securing your first career employment following college graduation. Congratulations!

Of course, after several months of networking, sending out more resumés than you care to think about, having some interviews, and one or two "nibbles" from prospective employers, this may not appear to be all that great an adventure after all.

Has it occurred to you that what you are doing now may actually be more difficult than the work you will be doing after somebody hires you to work for them? It could well be true. The important thing is to realize that, for now, your job is to find and *secure* your first real career position — not just a job. The truth is that it will likely take you longer than it did your counterparts a decade ago. Such is the state of the post-graduation career market in the mid- to late-1990s.

The July 12, 1993, issue of *Fortune* magazine reported on the economy and job prospects for graduating seniors saying, [both] "have been bleak for four years running. All the numbers are down; total job offers, offers per graduate, recruiter visits per campus, number of campuses visited, starting salaries."

The *Fortune* article added that, "Recession and restructuring have done more than cut the jobs available to seniors.

They have permanently changed the way graduates and employers seek each other out. Students unaware of these changes — or unwilling to play by a new set of rules — are striking out cold."

That's why this book was written. To give you an edge in locating employment in a tight and changing job market. To give you the skills in career management that will be vital to you, not just now, but throughout your working life.

Drake Beam Morin is uniquely equipped to assist you in your first career job search. Founded in 1967, the Company has become the world's leading provider of career transition services with more than 150 offices on six continents. The firm employs a full-time staff of more than 500 professionals with relevant backgrounds in business and the behavioral sciences which has led the way in developing job search and career transition training materials as well as a unique library of videotapes.

The Drake Beam Morin Guide to Getting Started With Your Career is designed to be a lifelong career tool. It is a comprehensive, reality-based and results-oriented resource for securing your first career employment today and, should it become necessary, a refresher for locating successive positions later on.

This is the beginning. You can make it a good one. Good luck!

New York City, July 14, 1993

Personal assessment

What do you really want to do?

"What do you want to be when you grow up?" It's an old joke among adults who have already spent years in the workplace. The inference is that the person asked the question has *not* really found his or her way as an adult. And, while you may not always feel like it, you *are* grown up — at least in the eyes of modern society — with a college degree and very likely in debt for that education. And you now find yourself with economic as well as both family and peer pressures to get on with your life.

It has been said that the ideal vocation is something you'd do anyway — whether or not you were paid for your time and effort. That may sound a bit altruistic, but chances are, it hits very close to the truth of the matter. We all know people who struggle on in jobs they truly dislike, but fear quitting because they need the income. How sad! And, how essential to avoid such a situation.

You *can* avoid such a prospect by choosing your career carefully — weighing your abilities, your interests, experience, and even your passions in life — then matching all that with the constellation of career possibilities that exist today. Your educational background is important, but it need not be an absolute in determining your livelihood. Many career options are open to the educated person who is eager to learn and to grow in a position. This is especially true for liberal arts graduates and those with degrees in the social sciences. The exact subject matter you have studied may be less important than the study habits, skills, and experience you gained either in the classroom and laboratory or while working during your college years.

Drake Beam Morin's Dr. Marcia Fox, author of *Put Your Degree to Work*,[1] said in a recent interview, "I began working last spring with two very bright seniors who were about to graduate. And the experience truly disturbed me. These kids were *paralyzed*. They didn't have a *clue* what they wanted to do with their lives. Of course, all the bad news about the present job market no doubt had a lot to do with their inability to make decisions. But, it was even worse than that. They didn't know where to begin. And, it's very difficult to help people who can't even begin to tell you what they *might* like to do!"

If you feel that description typifies your feelings and fears (or comes anywhere close), there are a number of excellent resources that can help you identify your strengths, interests, and abilities. However, please note that many of the instruments listed below, while not available to the individual, may be accessed through a college career office, an educational or testing psychologist, or another career professional. Also, it is important to realize that the results of many of these same inventory instruments should only be interpreted by a trained, even a certified, professional.

The Myers-Briggs Type Indicator is a self-administered multiple-choice survey which illuminates your personality type — whether you're introverted or extroverted, fact-based or intuitive, analytical or emotional. This tool can help you better understand your special strengths, and the type of work you might enjoy and be successful in doing.

The Campbell Interest and Skill Survey, is a measure of self-reported interests and skills. It's major purpose is to help individuals understand how their interest and skills map into the occupational world, thereby helping them make better career choices

1. W. W. Norton & Company, New York, 1988

John L. Holland's *Self-directed Search*[2] (SDS) is a comprehensive vocational interest inventory which may help lead you to a career choice or confirm an occupational preference. *The Occupations Finder*, a part of SDS, lists 1,346 occupations which include all of the most common occupations in the United States in the late 1980s. A companion *Dictionary of Occupational Titles* (DOT), which can be found in most libraries, employment and college career centers, presents descriptions of occupations and estimates of interests, aptitudes, and educational requirements associated with each one.

Discover is a computer-based program available at many college and university career centers and at public libraries which have career divisions. *Discover* contains extensive information on some 450 different occupations. By interacting with this computer program, you can move through a step-by-step exercise in career decision making — gaining valuable knowledge about your interests, values, and abilities.

The Occupational Outlook Handbook, updated biennially by the Bureau of Labor Statistics of the U. S. Department of Labor, lists more than 200 occupations and such descriptions as the nature of the work, working conditions, present employment, training requirements, job outlook, and typical earnings for each.

Again, however, be aware that experts warn against doing your career assessment strictly on your own. They point out that you can get bogged down or confused by the results. Many find their career options and inclinations become much clearer when working with a professional career counselor. Many college and university Career Centers employ such professionals and offer their services at no cost or for a reasonable fee to students and alumni. If you have left school, you can locate local job counseling services in your telephone company's Yellow Pages. Or, if you prefer, you can contact the National Board for Certified Counselors for a listing of certified career counselors in your area. Their address is:

2. Psychological Assessment Resources, Inc., Odessa, FL, 1990

National Board for Certified Counselors
3D Terrace Way
Greensboro, NC 27403
(910) 547-0607

After you've been tested, examined, checked, and certified... after you've run the computer programs and read the literature...you still have the decision to make: Where does the rest of your life begin? What are you going to do now that you're no longer a student?

The noted independent career consultant Howard Figler, writing in *CPC Annual* (published by the Career Placement Council), offered the following encouragement concerning career choices:

"With your multiple skills and interests, you may be attracted to many different jobs, careers, industries, and organizations. The map of possible choices is so large that some people are driven to psychological tests, Ouija boards, advice-giving relatives, mountain top gurus, and horoscopes as sources of wisdom. Can some 'expert' get a better grip on a good career choice for you than you can?" He answers, NO.

How can you then manage the career choice process yourself? Figler suggests that "Lightning will not flash and a voice say to you, 'Go, thou, forth and do _____.' But you can get your best clues by answering the following:

"1. When have you felt most energized, most filled with purpose and motivation? Identify two or more occasions in your life when you were fully involved, rolling along, getting things done.

"2. What are you doing when you are most comfortable with yourself? What kinds of activities seem just right for you?

"3. What sort of service or product do you believe people have too little of and that you can help provide?

"4. What kind of work would you regard as a personal challenge for you, an opportunity to test yourself, something to do better than has been done by others before you?

"5. When in your life have you felt most respected, most valued for your work, whether paid or unpaid?"

Figler concludes, "If you can answer even one of the above questions, you have a clue about where you should be looking, the kind of work that would draw on your best efforts. Your skills, interests, values, traits, etc., can then be used to support your work goals."

As Figler suggests, you must make sure you're in charge of your own "Ship of State." There is a major decision to be made here, and you are the only human being in the world who has the right to make it — or who *should*. Some are sure to disagree with your decision. Good. That shows you're thinking for yourself, because friends and family always want to try to "protect" us from bad decisions and missed opportunities. If they disagree, let them. This is *your* life, remember. Of course, if many people disagree with your decision, take careful note of their objections. What they say may not change your mind, but at least you'll have a clearer idea of the possible negatives.

Politicians talk about a good candidate's having "fire in the belly." Without one, they say no one will make it as an elected public servant. Can you identify your own, personal and unique "fire in the belly"? What really gets your juices flowing? What are you truly passionate about? And, as was suggested earlier in this chapter, "What would you do if money were not a consideration?"

If you can give an answer to these questions, if you can put a name on the career that would fulfill you in all these ways, then you are probably close to an answer. Of course, it's important that there be open positions in this field and that it gives you the chance to earn enough money to meet your lifestyle goals. If it happens to be a career that you are not presently qualified for, then get more education or training or whatever it takes to *be* qualified. As the popular sports shoe advertising says, "Just *do* it!"

So what if others advise against whatever it is that "lights your fire"? So what if you might not make a "go" of it the first time? As a young adult, a few early "missteps" are not going to wreck your career, especially if you learn from your errors. So what if you don't have all the resources you think you need? So what if people say you're too young? Too inexperienced? As Figler noted, "Ah, mere trifles. The Ship of State moves ahead."

Big firm or small company?
Once you've decided *what* to do, the next logical question is often, "Where to do it?" We're not referring to geography here — you probably already have a good idea in whih part of the country you want to work. This refers to the size organization you want to join. There *are* relative merits to companies of every size — the large corporate entity, the mid-size firm, and even the small shop of fewer than 50 people...in many cases, a *lot* fewer than 50.

It's a good idea to recall the recent past: mergers, acquisitions, and the attendant downsizing that has inevitably followed ownership changes among large companies makes them far less stable employers than they once were. Huge layoffs are announced with alarming regularity. And, corporate debt has ballooned — all making job security within many of the Fortune 500 a dim memory.

However, between 1988 and 1992, small companies — those employing fewer than 500 people — added all of the net new jobs in the United States. According to Anthony P. Carnevale, Executive Director of the Institute for Workplace Learning in Alexandria, Virginia, five out of every six American workers now earn paychecks from companies with fewer than a thousand employees.[3]

Many agree this is where the immediate future lies — with the smaller firm. "The opportunities are with new, small, up-and-coming companies," according to Karen B. Andrews, Career Services Director at Kennesaw State College in Marietta, Georgia.[4] Of course, available

3. *America and the New Economy*, Jossey-Bass, 1991
4. *National Business Employment Weekly*, Special College Career Edition, Fall 1992

positions in these firms will be fewer per company, but the competition for those positions may also be less than within larger firms.

Few small or middle size companies — and almost assuredly no small size firms — have the personnel or resources to recruit on campus. So, unless someone in your family or close circle of friends owned or worked in one, you may have little information about the benefits — and the possible drawbacks — of working for a smaller company.

Students sometimes have the image of the small firm as a mom-and-pop operation where members of the family run everything and new hires are overworked and underpaid. However, the *National Business Employment Weekly* has reported that this impression is unfounded and that the part about being overworked and underpaid may actually be more applicable to large companies.

Many who *do* work for smaller firms indicate that they have the opportunity to perform a wide variety of tasks and assume greater responsibilities early in their careers. The very nature of small companies rewards the generalist rather than the specialist. This gives new employees the opportunity to gain valuable hands-on experience, mastering a diversity of skills early on. This can be a boon to their careers.

Interestingly, entry-level positions within smaller organizations often pay surprisingly well — often at least on par with similar positions in much larger companies. True, the benefits may be fewer, and there may be less *perceived* job security than with a very large firm. However, one must ask just how much job security there is today in a firm of *any* size.

Also, though these firms may not offer much in the way of training programs, it is also true that larger companies, which once had extensive, formal training for entry level personnel, have been cutting back these programs in recent years, placing new employees in more productive positions much sooner.

One of the benefits of working for the smaller employer is the opportunity to develop close, personal, and caring relationships with one's fellow workers — even with the managers and owners of the company. Recent college graduates who miss the collegiality of the campus may find the close-knit environment within the small company much more comfortable than the comparatively sterile, much more formal atmosphere of a firm employing thousands.

Though few small companies recruit on campus, as noted earlier, many do rely on college placement offices for resumé referrals and to post job listings. Networking, however, is likely the most productive avenue for locating a position with a smaller employer.

Conducting a national job search among smaller companies is still possible. The following reference books provide an excellent resource:

The Hidden Job Market (1991, Peterson's) lists 2,000 fast-growing high-tech companies.

Ward's Business Directory of U.S. Private and Public Companies (1992, Gale Research) is a guide to 133,000 companies — 90% of which are privately owned.

America's Fastest Growing Employers (1992, Bob Adams) profiles 700 high-growth organizations.

Corporate Technology Directory - 1992 Edition (Corporate Technology Information Services) lists 35,000 high-tech companies including 22,000 that employ fewer than one thousand people each.[5]

---

5. *National Business Employment Weekly*, Special Fall 1992 Edition

Working in the 90's:
The changing nature of work
and the workplace

Career prospects today: What's hot and what's not

The Bureau of Labor Statistics (BLS) of the U. S. Department of Labor estimates that today's college graduate entering the work force will change careers four times during his or her working life. Change *careers*, not just jobs! Further, based on experience with more than one million clients over a quarter century, Drake Beam Morin estimates that the average professional person will change *jobs* eight times during a working lifetime.

The advantage in this forecast is that you are not likely making the same type of long-term commitment your parents made. (Or thought they were making!) Although you now have to make up your mind to seek career employment in one field or another, it isn't a decision you will have to live with for the rest of your life. Experts say that many of today's graduates entering the labor force could well end their careers working in a discipline which may not even exist today. Consider such recent developments as genetic engineering, virtual reality, and multi-media computer applications. As recently as the early 1980s these would have been considered the stuff of science fiction. Yet, today, these new disciplines are earning high profits and are poised for exponential growth.

Who can say what any of us will be doing 20 years from now? The discipline which may propel you into your prime earning years may not have been invented yet! In fact, the Labor Department states that, by the year 2000, one-half of today's workforce will be in jobs that haven't been invented yet.

For now, however, the object of the exercise is to secure employment in a career which your education, experience, and interests have prepared you for. For most graduates, that means choosing a field which exists *today* and which enables you to develop the skills and experience which will be most in demand *tomorrow*.

You have no doubt heard that the U. S. has been moving toward a service economy for a couple of decades. The decline of this country's manufacturing base indicates that the best prospects for the near future lie in industries and organizations that *do* things rather than *make* things. In 1993 service businesses account for three-quarters of the U. S. Gross Domestic Product (GDP). "In the future," according to Lord William Rees-Mogg, the former editor of the *Times* of London, "more business will be based on intangibles than on tangibles."

Along these lines, *Tomorrow's Jobs,* a pamphlet reprinted from the Labor Department's Occupational Outlook Handbook (printed annually), suggests that "service-producing industries — including transportation, communications, and utilities; retail and wholesale trade; services; government; and finance, insurance, and real estate — are expected to account for approximately 23 million of the 24.6 million new jobs created between 1990 and the year 2005. To put that number in perspective, a total of 33 million jobs were created during the 15 years from 1975 to 1990.

"In addition," the publication notes, "the services division within this sector — which includes health, business and educational services — contains 16 of the 20 fastest growing industries, and 12 of the 20 industries adding the most jobs. Expansion of service sector employment is linked to...

changes in consumer tastes and preferences, legal and regulatory changes, advances in science and technology, and changes in the way businesses are organized and managed."

Employment within the services division is expected to grow by 34.7 percent by 2005, accounting for almost one-half of all new jobs. The two largest industry groups in this division — health services (nursing and other specialties) and business services — are projected to continue very rapid growth. Computer programming and other computer technology-related jobs are also expected to grow. Social, legal, engineering, and management services industries illustrate the service division's strong growth for the future.

The Department of Labor offers the following forecasts for other service-oriented industries during the period from 1990 through the year 2005:

Retail trade employment up by 26 percent; wholesale trade to increase by 16 percent.

Finance, insurance, and real estate employment — increasing by 21 percent.

Employment in transportation, communications, and public utilities — up by 15 percent.

Government employment — excluding public education and public hospitals — is expected to increase 14 percent.

Among goods-producing industries, overall employment is not expected to show any appreciable change though growth prospects within this sector vary considerably.

The construction industries are expected to be the only goods-producing industry where employment will increase. The gain through 2005 is projected to be 18 percent.

Manufacturing employment is expected to decline by three percent from the 1990s level of 19.1 million workers. Further, the composition of manufacturing employment is expected to shift in that most of the disappearing jobs will be in production. However, the number of professional, technical, and managerial positions in manufacturing companies will increase.

Mining employment is expected to decline by six percent.

Overall employment in agriculture, forestry, and fishing has been declining for decades and is expected to continue — by six percent through 2005.

To summarize, the greatest growth potential in the American job market through the middle of the next decade lies in such services as health care and business services — where almost half of all new jobs will be created. Job growth among goods-producing industries appears bleak except for construction industries.

However, most of the jobs that become available over the next decade or so won't be created by an increase in the size of the total work force. The Labor Department forecasts that most jobs will be born of replacement needs. This means that even occupations with little or no employment growth — or slower than average employment growth — may still offer many job openings. Replacement openings occur as people leave their occupations — some to transfer to other occupations as a step up the career ladder or to change careers. Others stop working in order to return to school, assume household responsibilities, or to retire.

Occupations with high replacement openings are generally within large employment groups where pay, status, and training requirements are all low, and where the proportion of young and part-time workers is high. Occupations with relatively few replacement openings tend to be those with high pay, status, and training requirements. These same low replacement occupations tend to have high proportions of prime working age, full-time workers. Among professional specialty occupations, for example, only 46 percent of total job opportunities will result from replacement needs.

This suggests that well-educated, highly paid people tend

to hold onto their jobs longer. As this is the type of position you aspire to, and because the ranks of these well-educated job holders have been swelled by the so-called "Baby Boom" generation, you will be competing for fewer openings than this earlier generation. This means a successful job search today requires more energy, flexibility, and strategizing on your part. But the results will be worth it.

Robert O. Snelling, Sr., and Anne M. Snelling first published their valuable employment resource book, *Jobs! What they are...Where they are...What they pay!*[6] in 1985, updating it in 1989 and 1992. The authors identify the seven top career areas with the best entry-level jobs as:

Computers — especially service technicians and systems analysts

Engineering — biomedical, chemical, and both electrical and electronic engineering positions have excellent potential

Finance — with good entry-level positions available for junior analysts, securities sales representatives, banking trainees, claims representatives, and accountants

Health Services and Technology — with nurses, physical therapists, electrocardiograph technicians, and radiologic technologists mentioned as promising careers for those at the entry level

Marketing — a career area where junior copywriters, junior analysts, and public relations assistants are considered promising positions

Media and Communications — where broadcast technicians and news assistants are recommended positions

Sales — a broad area with openings in virtually every career field. The Snellings particularly mention advertising and computer sales representatives; direct sales, food sales, manufacturers' sales representatives; and insurance agents as positions with promise for those just entering the work force

6. Fireside, New York, 1992

John Youngblood, Assistant Director of Atlanta's Emory University Career Center, offers this assessment of "what's hot and what's not" for 1993:

"Computer information systems are hot for computer science majors. Organizations calling all the time with listings for students in these areas.

"And the Allied Health field is still a popular area. In terms of our liberal arts students, training programs with brokerage firms are fewer this year. Banking and insurance are also two of the leaders. And many of our students are going into education.

"A new program called Teach for America seems to fit many of our Emory students' criteria because they want to go back to graduate school in a couple of years. Teach for America is a private two year program which doesn't require a teaching certificate. It allows the graduate to teach in an inner city or rural locale for two years, then return to graduate school.

"Teach for America is backed by a non-profit organization that's about four years old. It operates like the Peace Corps, but for the educational system in this country. They select the brightest students they can find who have always been successful and send them into schools whose students have not experienced much success before. This program is really a challenge for the graduates and very good for the school systems.

"Journalism and publishing are not hot right now. Interestingly enough, the public relations field is wide open for those who want to intern; there just isn't much hiring in that field. They want people to intern, but the jobs are limited."

Mr. Youngblood concludes, "We have a new major at Emory called International Studies which is producing many students who are interested in using their language skills. But, unless graduates are going to the D.C. area, it is very hard to find openings for them at the bachelor's level."

What employers are looking for

The Northwestern Lindquist-Endicott Report —1993[7], written by Northwestern University's Director of Placement, Victor R. Lindquist, is more targeted toward the number of college graduates being hired for particular types of positions than the broader forecasts by the Bureau of Labor Statistics. This report annually surveys 258 well-known business and industrial organizations. It cites the following changes in actual and anticipated employment of inexperienced bachelor's and master's graduates by those firms for 1992 and '93:

The employment of inexperienced college graduates during 1992 and for 1993 as reported by 258 companies

Bachelor's Level

Number of:	1992		1993	
	Companies	Grads	Companies	Grads
Engineering	119	4,560	120	5,044
Accounting	96	6,040	84	6,074
Sales-Marketing	64	863	55	857
Business Admin.	81	1,603	73	1,748
Liberal Arts*	61	1,226	56	1,154
Computer*	79	1,891	75	2,238
Chemistry*	27	330	23	350
Math or Statistics	33	414	31	487
Economics* or Finance	66	906	56	904
Other Fields/ Undesignated	58	1,469	47	1,470
Totals - Bachelor's Level		**19,302**		**20,326**

* In considering the overall demand for graduates in the liberal arts, the asterisked (*) disciplines must also be recognized, since these courses are usually offered in colleges of arts and sciences.

7. The Placement Center of Northwestern University, Evanston, IL, 1992

Companies hiring and master's graduates hired:

Master's Level

Number of:	1992		1993	
	Companies	Grads	Companies	Grads
Engineering	68	732	52	715
Other Technical Fields	33	375	28	391
MBA with Technical BS	51	793	51	905
MBA with Nontechnical BA	92	1,496	87	1,546
Accounting	20	1,584	12	562
Other Fields/Undesignated	19	308	14	252
Total - Master's Level		**5,288**		**4,371**

Summary of Change in Demand for 1993

Engineering: Bachelor's - Up for 1993	11%
Master's - Down for 1993	2%
Non-engineering: Bachelor's - Up for 1993	4%
Master's - Down for 1993	20%
Total: Bachelor's - Up for 1993	5%
Master's - Down for 1993	17%

The Northwestern Lindquist-Endicott Report for 1993
pointed toward trends which are expected to continue
well into the decade of the 90's:

Career opportunities are mixed

Almost half of companies surveyed plan to increase
hiring of bachelor candidates

Hiring of engineers will increase while hiring of non-
engineering majors will decline

Almost half of companies surveyed are looking for fewer
graduates than in recent years

Hiring plans for master's graduates will decline with most
of the loss in Accounting

Students will have to market themselves effectively and
with flexibility

The job of choice may be in another location or at a level
less than desired

The outlook is not one of desperation but of competition that requires a foundation in good planning and assertive action.

Demise of the paternalistic employer

In a companion Drake Beam Morin book, *Managing Stress in Turbulent Times*, those already in the workplace are reminded that, "The days in which employers 'took care' of their employees in a paternalistic fashion are long gone. No one today realistically expects he or she has a job 'for life.' Increasingly today, employees are expected to manage their own careers and to align their skills and objectives to those of the organization. The only real certainty is *change* — and the rewards that will accrue to those with the ability to flex, to gain new skills, and to use existing skills in different environments and for different applications."

In her book, *The Smith College Job Guide*,[8] Elizabeth Tener counsels that "Job security is an illusion. Back in the forties, fifties and sixties, when the U.S. economy was the strongest in the world and social change was slower, a company made a tacit agreement with anyone it hired to keep him or her on indefinitely. As long as you performed adequately, you could count on [having] a job.

"Company and worker loyalty," she concludes, "are largely things of the past." She points out that even larger companies are fighting for their lives today in a world of global competition, buyouts and fluctuating economic conditions. What if your company merges with another one and your job is redundant? Will you be retained or released? Cutbacks today are commonplace. In the first half of 1993, major computer companies, auto manufacturers and aerospace firms announced the furloughs of more than 100,000 workers and the permanent dissolution of tens of thousands of other jobs.

Though company managers might want to "take care" of their subordinates, they can't afford to be sentimental. And, neither can the employees. In the increasingly uncertain and competitive world of the 90's, an employee

8. Penguin Books, New York, 1991

is simply operating in his or her own informed self-interest by keeping an eye out for corporate distress inside the organization and for better opportunities outside.

There is no doubt that the decline of company loyalty has increased feelings of uncertainty and anxiety among employees. But, there is also a positive side to the situation. Looking for new employment no longer imputes incompetence to the job-seeker. And job-hopping — once considered a sign of instability — is no longer so considered, especially when the hops are a planned part of one's own career management. It is simply one of today's realities to realize that a career is not a single job. Further, today's new graduates should probably *not* count on careers with the firms that offer them their first positions. "All the more reason," Tener concludes, "to learn how to crack the job market, to uncover hidden jobs, and to present yourself as a strong, reliable candidate to someone who might want to hire you."

What more can you do?

With competition for entry-level positions becoming greater every year, many are finding that sometimes "little things mean a lot." Having two applicants for the same position — recent graduates with virtually identical academic scores and backgrounds — savvy employers may look beyond courses and obvious qualifications to help them decide whom to hire. For example...

Internships. This says that you know something about the world of work but, more important, it says you know something about their business if you have interned with a firm in their field. The *Fortune* article mentioned in the Foreword suggests that, because companies can't afford to hire duds, "...openings for grads often aren't being filled by strangers. They're being filled by people hand-picked well before graduation. Bill Dittmore, Director of Recruitment and College Relations for General Mills, says, 'About a third of our offers to new grads go to people who've already worked for us as interns. We plan to raise that to between 40% and 50%.' By making offers to people already familiar with the company, Dittmore gets a higher acceptance rate and lower turnover." If you haven't served an internship yet, it may not be too late to have one. Why not use the summer immediately following graduation? If you don't have a regular, paying position lined up, what else are you going to be doing that would be more important?

Published papers. Whether in scholarly journals or even in industry trade papers, publication credit sets you apart from everyone else. Again, it may not be too late to get in print. And researching and writing something for the field you hope to join may prove to be a very worthwhile counterpart to your summer job search.

Neatness counts. Your professors may never have been sticklers for the visual appearance or style of your papers and other academic work products. Don't count on that being the case in the race for a quality position that pays well. Check every cover letter and resumé for details. Correct spelling and punctuation, the agreement of subjects and predicates, and an appealing overall visual impression of yourself on paper all go a long way to saying, "This is a person who is serious about doing the job right the first time."

Present yourself professionally in person, too. Of course you're going to wear your "earnest" suit to interviews. But, again, look at the details. The cleanliness and grooming of one's hair and nails make an important first impression on employers and their representatives. Recently shined shoes also count. It may seem picayune to you; but, to those on the other side of the desks, it says something about self-discipline and self-worth. Of course, a nice suit and good grooming won't get you a job. But your failure to observe these basics could eliminate you from further interviews and the opportunity to present your skills.

Watch what you say. Remember that interviews don't end when the interviewer puts the pen down and closes the notebook. Those unguarded moments are often the most telling ones of all about a job candidate. There is nothing "off the record" in these situations. So, if you don't want it to be remembered and, perhaps, "played back" later on, don't say it. Interviewers aren't your friends — not yet, anyway. And much of their job is the disqualification of candidates. Don't give them that chance with a thoughtless or mean-spirited comment.

There is an old saying, "What you are speaks so loudly I can't hear what you're saying." In today's employment climate perhaps more than at any time in the recent past, it's important to project a professional image all the time you're "on" in front of a potential employer. Interviewers often make judgments of an applicant's suitability based on the first minute or two of observation and interaction. Once you've passed this "initial inspection," what you say becomes increasingly important. If you fail that initial inspection, what you say will be discounted or ignored. In fact, you will have been eliminated; the rest of the interview, no matter how polite, will be nothing more than a formality.

Your career planning and placement office

Its role and responsibilities

The role of the college Career Center or Placement Office has been changing rather dramatically in recent years. Donald A. Casella, director of the Career Center and associate vice president for student affairs at San Francisco State University, writes that "The basic and fundamental purpose of our services was once 'Job Placement.' Later, our root rationale became 'Career Planning.' Now we find ourselves irrevocably involved in 'Networking' as our fundamental reason for existence."[9]

He contends that the college placement or career office is becoming a major "intersection" where 1) students and alumni, 2) employers, and 3) faculty and staff meet to deal with many types of career matters today.

"Today," Dr. Casella writes, "bottom-line success is becoming increasingly more dependent upon how well we serve as three-way information crossroads. Our activities rise from our serving new basic concepts that involve information management, connecting, linking, networking, communicating, contacts, partnerships, co-sponsorships, cooperativeness...indeed, such basics are both our most important services and the most effective strategies for delivering them. For our purposes," he concludes, "...the evolving career center paradigm may be defined as: 'Network,' the combined

9. *Journal of the College Placement Council,* Summer 1990

23

verb and noun meaning both 'to associate actively with...' and 'an active association of...human, print, and electronic career resources.'"

Networking is regarded as the most efficient and effective method of performing both the job placement and career planning activities required by today's college students, graduates, and alumni.

The College Placement Council — the association serving collegiate career centers — conducts a quadrennial survey of its 1,518 member offices nationwide. Those responding to this most recent audit (823 or 54.2%) provided the following overview of services offered by such organizations nationally. The results of the previous survey are included for comparison purposes:

Services offered through career planning and placement centers

	Percent of Respondents	
	1987	**1991**
Career counseling	94.1	94.2
Occupational and employer information library	93.6	93.7
Placement of graduates into full-time employment	96.8	93.4
Campus interviewing	96.5	91.6
Placement of students into summer and part-time jobs	87.0	83.2
Placement of alumni	88.9	82.7
Credential service	76.4	71.9
Resumé referral	74.2	71.6
Cooperative education, intern, experiential program	53.7	62.8
Resumé booklets	56.3	56.3
Vocational testing	53.2	52.1
Computerized candidate data base	—	48.2
Career planning or employment readiness course for credit	32.1	31.6
Academic counseling	33.0	28.7
Dropout prevention and counseling	19.9	16.2

Recruiting activities

	1987	1991
Allowed employers to prescreen job candidates	81.4	71.6
Sponsored career days	64.0	68.0
Sponsored job fairs	44.9	61.0
Worked directly with third-party recruiters	46.0	44.8
Informed employers of their services through mass mailings, phone calls, personalized letters and visits	yes	yes
Fewer companies recruiting on campus vs. previous year	—	54.3

About a third of the respondents charge students specific fees for services, and 36% charge alumni such fees. More than one-fifth (22%) charge employers for specific services (up from 9% in 1987) — primarily for participation in career days and fairs.

On average, according to this 1991 survey, almost 63 percent of the graduating class use the career planning and placement office, 36.6 percent obtain jobs through the office, and almost 19 percent get jobs through on-campus recruitment.

The greatest problem reported by the placement center offices was budget and staff constraints. Clearly, the majority of such offices are doing their best to do a great deal with insufficient resources.

John Youngblood, the Emory University Career Center assistant director quoted earlier, reflected on the role of his office saying, "Our Career Center is very much a counseling and training office for Emory students. Unlike ours, other college and university placement offices focus on specialty areas such as MBA and Law School graduates. You don't find a lot of undergraduate liberal arts colleges that have a traditional 'placement' office where all they do is on-campus recruiting and other traditional placement functions."

New ways of assisting students and employers
"We like to become involved with our students very early on in their college careers. A career decision is really a lifelong process. It's never too early to start exploring career areas. By doing that over the course of four years, the student is able to make a better decision rather than just starting that process in the senior year. We're very big in promoting experiential education and learning opportunities. By that, we mean internships and 'shadowing' opportunities with organizations and alumni in the community. These give students the chance actually to experience a career area — to get out of the classroom and into the 'real world.' We have an extensive internship program that we rely heavily on.

"A lot of organizations," he continues, "are changing their focus in terms of on-campus recruiting. We have more companies coming on campus to recruit juniors and sometimes even sophomores for extensive internships and internship training programs. Procter & Gamble is an example of a company that's changing its philosophy in the way it recruits. They used to recruit seniors very heavily for their management and sales training programs. Now they are beginning to put heavy emphasis on recruiting juniors to get them in for a summer internship so they can actually preview some of these potential hires for a full summer. This gives both the company and the student more information about the other.

"We also do a lot in networking — making connections possible for students, teaching them how the job search works, how to ask questions, how to get into organizations. The way into an organization almost always used to be through the human resources department. Sometimes that's still the case. But organizations are less and less 'top down' hierarchical. As Phil Gardner of Michigan State says, 'More and more organizations are like a spider web where there are many different entry points.' We want to educate people in terms of ways to enter that web. So we're serving an educational function here. And we're doing this through a variety of workshops and individual counseling. The latter is often the most effective because people are coming from a different point in their own career search.

"We realize that a lot of the hiring opportunities today are not in the large organizations as they used to be, but in smaller organizations. This presents some different challenges to career and placement centers in terms of what they can do to assist the student. Organizations no longer have the staff or the time to recruit on campus as they used to do. So our job now is to get out and do more marketing of our services and our students to these organizations — making it possible for them to learn about our students without having to come on campus.

"We're in a transition right now trying to find new ways to network, to get involved with the middle and smaller size organizations. We're meeting with our Alumni Clubs this summer around the country to give our graduates a means for giving something back to the college instead of just giving money. We're hoping they'll be able to help us by sponsoring career days and provide career information for students and graduating seniors."

Clearly, the role of the college career planning and placement center has changed substantially in the past couple of decades, and that role is still evolving. The emphasis today is more and more on information exchange — using all the means possible to inform students, alumni, faculty, and employers of each other's needs, capabilities, and offerings. Innovation and, especially, computerization have changed the way both the career office and its clients work.

However, one thing is still as true today as it ever was: your college career center can only assist you in finding a position. It can't give you a job or get one for you.

You are still the only one who can do that.

Assessing today's job market

Research is a key

Looking for your first career position after college is a lot like selling a new product. In this case, *you* are the product!

To market yourself, you have to learn all you can about your customers (your potential employers), where they're located, and what they will pay you for your "product." You also need to know how to appeal to them to your maximum advantage. To develop this "marketing" — in your case, job search — strategy, you should be able to answer the following questions:

What kinds of companies or industries are interested in your skills?

What is the title of the person who can actually hire you? Do you need to be interviewed by the Vice President for Finance? The Regional Sales Manager? The Human Resources Director? Someone else?

Where are the firms that interest you located? Do they have local, regional, or national offices? Which office should you approach to get the job you want? Who is the individual you have to see to get that position?

How can you best make contact with these "prospect" firms? Through your personal network? Search firms? Blanket distribution of resumés? Or through direct contact with the company by letter and telephone follow-up?

Which of your qualities (education, experience, skills, personality, etc.) will make you especially interesting to these firms?

What is the general salary range for the position you seek? How does that range relate to the salaries for entry-level positions in other types of business, and for other types of careers?

At the beginning of your job search, it's important to make a realistic assessment of the size of the market you're approaching. Are you limiting your market to a local or regional area? What are the trade-offs in broadening your market...or restricting it? These assessments are essential to designing a realistic marketing effort that will produce the results you seek.

It's essential to do this research first — before you make contact in the marketplace. By doing this "homework," you'll have current knowledge of relevant industry trends and company reputations. These are important pluses because, in all your contacts with potential employers, it will be clear to each interviewer, phone contact, and recipient of your letters that your interest in the company is backed by true initiative and solid preparation.

The following section contains information on three vital aspects of the research process:

What to research: the general kinds of information you need to gather

Index of research sources: the many sources available to you that can provide valuable information for assessing a job

Finding answers to commonly asked questions — which sources to go to for answers to an assortment of questions

What to research
As you target an industry and specific companies, you need to get as much information as possible about that industry, individual organizations, the position of each

firm within the industry, and the names of individuals you plan to contact in each organization. These are some of the kinds of information that will prove helpful to you:

Industry information

- Historic trends

- Recent trends

- Noteworthy companies within the industry

Specific company information

- Its history, size, growth rate

- Its profitability

- Products and services

- Financial history and current status

- Top management players — their backgrounds, tenure, and average age

- The company's culture

- Recent changes in company structure

- Changes in product or service lines

Geographic area job trends

Index of research sources

There are a number of business directories that can be useful in planning your strategy to locate the right position. The directories listed below can be found at most public, college, university, and business libraries. In many urban areas, local directories are published by the Chamber of Commerce and governmental agencies.

Before using any directory, however, read its Preface and Table of Contents. This will save you time and indicate the most efficient way to locate the information you need.

Guide to American Directories, B. Klein Publications, P. O. Box 8503, Coral Springs, FL 33065.

A listing and description of 6,000 directories with more than 300 major industrial, professional, and mercantile classifications.

Useful in locating membership names and titles.

Encyclopedia of Associations - Volume One: National Organizations of the United States, Gale Research Company, Book Tower, Detroit, MI 48266.

A guide to 14,000 national organizations of all types, purposes and interests. Gives name and headquarters addresses; telephone numbers; chief officials; number of members; staffs and chapters; descriptions of membership, programs, and activities. Includes lists of special committees and departments, publications, and a three-year convention schedule. Cross-indexed.

Useful in locating placement committees which can help you learn of specific job openings in your field of interest; getting membership lists of individuals in order to develop personal contacts; learning where and when conferences are being held.

Standard and Poor's Register of Corporations, Directors and Executives, Standard and Poor, Inc., 345 Hudson Street, New York, NY 10014.

A guide to public companies in the U. S.
Volume I — Corporate Listings

Alphabetical listing (by business name) of 37,000 corporations — including address, telephone number, names and titles of officers and directors, public firms' Standard Industrial Classification codes (SIC) (for company/ industry cross referencing), annual sales, number of employees, some division names, principal and secondary businesses.

Volume II — Indexes
Section 1: SIC Index (green pages)

Section 2: SIC Codes (pink pages)
Provides a defined breakdown by line of business.

Section 3: Geographic Index (buff pages)
Lists companies in the Register by state and major cities.
Business names are alphabetical.

Section 4: Obituary Section (green pages)
Records of deaths in past year — providing decedents'
affiliations, business addresses, and dates of birth and
death.

Section 5: New Individual Additions (blue pages)
Alphabetical list of individuals appearing in the Register
for the first time, along with their principal business
connections and business addresses.

Section 6: New Company Additions (blue pages)
Alphabetical list of companies appearing in the Register
for the first time, includes their business address.

Standard and Poor's Register Supplement (Quarterly)
Gives revisions of corporate boards of directors, management executives and directors.

This is an updating of data for the other two volumes.

Dun & Bradstreet Million Dollar Directory - Volume I,
Dun & Bradstreet, Inc., 99 Church Street, New York,
NY 10007.

Similar to Standard and Poor's Register; however, this
single volume lists corporations with annual sales of
$1 million and more.

It is useful to use both Standard and Poor's and Dun
& Bradstreet together. One directory may include a
firm which the other does not — as well as additional
descriptions of products, subsidiaries, and officer titles.

Dun & Bradstreet Million Dollar Directory - Volume II, The Middle Market

Similar to S&P's Volume I and D&B Million Dollar Directory - Volume I, except this one only includes companies with a net worth of $500,000 to $999,999.

Dun & Bradstreet Reference Book of Corporate Managements

Contains data on directors and selected officers of 2,400 companies with annual sales of $20 million and up or which have 1,000 employees.

Information includes dates of birth, education, and business positions presently and previously held. For directors who are not officers, their present principal business connection is furnished.

Includes details of corporate officers which may not be included in other directories. Also gives the reader an idea of the personality of a corporation by providing information on the technical backgrounds of its officers.

Directory of Corporate Affiliations, National Register Publishing Company, Inc., 5201 Old Orchard Road, Skokie, IL 60076.

Provides detailed information on "who owns whom" as a result of mergers and acquisitions. Includes companies listed on the New York Stock Exchange, the American Stock Exchange, the "Fortune 500" and others — a total of 4,000 parent company listings.

This directory is useful when seeking detailed information on corporate structure of a parent company or for a company not listed in other directories because it is a subsidiary division or affiliate.

Standard Directory of Advertisers and Supplements, National Register Publishing Company, Inc.

Lists 17,000 companies doing national and regional advertising (including company name, phone number, products and services) as well as 80,000 executives and their titles, advertising agency handling each account, account executives, media used, and distribution.

Companies listed by product classification, alphabetical index, and trade name index.

A useful tool in locating marketing officers, names of parent companies, subsidiaries, and affiliates. A known trade name can be used to locate its manufacturer.

Standard Directory of Advertising Agencies, National Register Publishing Company, Inc.

Lists 4,400 agencies — 4,000 in U. S., 400 foreign.

Sections include:

Special Market Index
View at a glance of agencies specializing in Finance, Medicine, Resort and Travel, Black and Spanish Markets, Media Service Organizations, and Sales Promotion Agencies.

Media Services
Listing of sales promotion agencies, media services and time buying organizations, advertising agencies (including branches, personnel, and accounts arranged alphabetically), largest agencies (ranked by annual billings), geographical index of advertising agencies (listing names, addresses, and phone numbers of agencies by state and city).

Thomas Register of American Manufacturers, Thomas Publishing Company, One Penn Plaza, New York, NY 10001 (12 volumes).

Useful in locating many specific product manufacturers — large and small — not included in preceding directories.

Volumes 1-7
Products and services listed alphabetically. (Brand names and index in Volume 7.)

Volume 8
Company names, addresses, and telephone numbers listed alphabetically with branch offices, capital ratings, and company officials.

Volumes 9-12
Companies listed alphabetically and cross-indexed to the first eight volumes.

Polk's World Bank Directory — North American Edition
(U. S., Canada, Mexico, Central America, and Caribbean), R. L. Polk Company, 2001 Elm Hill Pike, P. O. Box 1340, Nashville, TN 37202.

A detailed listing of banks, other financial institutions, and government agencies by address. Also includes a geographic indexing with maps, names, and titles of officers.

Useful in researching corporations and government agencies.

Best's Insurance Reports, Property, and Casualty,
A. M. Best Company, Ambest Road, Oldwick, NJ 08858.

In-depth analyses, operating statistics, financial data, and officers of more than 1,300 major stock and mutual property-casualty insurance companies.

Also provides summary data on over 2,000 smaller mutual companies and 300 casualty companies operating in Canada.

Best's Insurance Reports, Life and Health

Supplies 1,250 individual company reports in addition to summary of 600 smaller companies similar to the property and casualty reports.

Corporate 10K Reports

Provide financial and historic information about a corporation. May be requested from each company's treasurer's office, public relations or public information office.

May also be available from public accounting firms, banks, and business, college and university libraries.

Prospectus

As a part of every public stock offering, a company's prospectus includes financial and historic data as well as information on the firm's directors, officers, and "insiders."

The Annual Report (Public companies only)

In addition to the balance sheet and the auditor's report, these documents also contain a letter from the chairman (and/or president) which usually reflects the firm's personality, well-being and direction.

In addition to the preceding research resources, there are many industry, Chamber of Commerce, and Fortune 500 directories, trade journals, annual reports and papers which may be found at your local business, college, university, and public libraries.

You may also find valuable corporate and industry information in the following:

• Business periodicals index

• Directory of Directors

• Reader's Guide to Periodical Literature

• The College Placement Annual

• Dictionary of Occupational Titles

• Encyclopedia of Careers and Vocational Guidance

• Occupational Outlook Handbook

• Directory of American Firms Operating in Foreign Countries

• Congressional Directory

• Congressional Yellow Book

- Federal Directory

- Federal Yellow Book

- Taylor's Encyclopedia of Government Officials

The following business-oriented magazines may also prove helpful:

- *Barron's*

- *Business Week*

- *Business World*

- *Forbes*

- *Fortune*

- *Inc.*

- *Money*

- *Nation's Business*

Resources for answering commonly asked questions

The following are the kinds of questions often asked by graduates seeking their first career positions. Each question is grouped with a list of sources where the answer may be found. The questions fall into four categories:

1. **Location**
2. **Industries**
3. **Companies**
4. **Employment Organizations**

Questions	Source for answers
1. Location	
What companies are nearby?	State industrial directories
	Dun & Bradstreet Reference Book of Corporate Managements
	Regional development agencies
	State and local Chambers of Commerce
In what state(s) does a company have facilities?	Moody's manuals
	Directory of Corporate Affiliates
	Company 10Ks and annual reports
2. Industries	
What are the high-growth industries today?	Value Line Investment Surveys
	Predicasts forecast manuals
	Refer to Directory of Industry Data Sources for other sources
What are the salary levels in specific industries?	American Compensation Association publications
	The American Almanac of Jobs and Salaries
	American Management Association surveys

Who are a firm's competitors?	Dun & Bradstreet Million Dollar Directory (list of other companies making same product)
	Standard and Poor's Industry Survey
	Business periodicals index
	Industry Buying Guides
What industries use specific types of professionals?	Encyclopedia of Associations
	National Trade and Professional Associations of the United States (identify appropriate organizations, obtain membership lists, note companies and industries)
	Directory of U. S. Labor Organizations (identify associations, obtain names of elected officials and department heads)
	Check your library for other occupational guidebooks.

3. Companies

How can I identify the products a company makes?	Company annual report
	Moody's manuals
	Thomas Register (company catalog volumes)
	U. S. Industrial Directory
What companies make certain products?	Thomas Register (product volumes)
	Dun & Bradstreet Million Dollar Directory
	Standard and Poor's Register of Corporations, Directors and Executives
	Standard Directory of Advertisers
How can I identify consulting organizations by their field?	Consultants and Consulting Organizations Directory (and companion directories)

40

There are also many industry-specific directories of consultants; see the Directory of Directories.

What are sources of company reports and analyses?	Standard and Poor's Stock Report
	Moody's Investors Fact Sheets
	Value Line Investment Surveys
	Wall Street Transcript
	Some libraries may subscribe to other stock analysis services.
What are management's practices concerning training?	Company annual reports (employee relations section)
	Membership directories for training organizations (e.g., American Society for Training and Development)
	The Career Guide — Dun's Employment Opportunities Directory
	Peterson's guides
Who are the key people in the company and what are their backgrounds?	Dun & Bradstreet Reference Book of Corporate Managements
	Standard and Poor's Register of Corporations, Directors and Executives
	Who's Who directories
	Corporate proxy statements
Who are the people in various lines of business?	Dun & Bradstreet American Corporate Families
	State industrial directories
	Company annual reports
	Other directories (refer to the Directory of Directories and Directory of Industry Data Sources for direction)

4. Employment Organizations

What are the names of employment agencies and/or executive recruiters?

The Directory of Executive Recruiters

Directories produced by state or local associations

How do I find out about government employment opportunities?

State: The State Administrative Officials Classified by Functions has a section listing state employment offices and their phone numbers.

Federal: the U. S. Office of Personnel Management (1900 E Street NW, Washington, D. C.) is responsible for nationwide recruiting for Civil Service positions at GS levels 1-15. This office also maintains a network of federal job information centers in major metro areas. Phone numbers are listed in the white pages of local telephone books under U. S. Government, Office of Personnel Management.

Job search strategies and skills

Networking and the informational interview
As you research industries and companies through the sources cited in the preceding chapter, you may well develop information that either confirms an earlier interest in a particular career or presents information about an industry and selected companies that pique your interest for the first time. Either will give you a general direction in which to begin moving — perhaps investigating several fields that are of interest to you. Your next step is to gain more insight into what the work is really like — the kinds of people you may be working with, the cultures of companies who employ people in these careers, and some of the issues facing those companies and their people today.

Perhaps the best way to gain these kinds of insights is through using your personal *network* to get informational interviews.

Informational interviews differ from actual employment interviews in several ways:

You are there earnestly seeking information, not to sell yourself.

This type interview will likely be easier to arrange than the job interview.

You're not being "graded" by a prospective employer, so you will probably be more at ease.

However, don't let the lack of pressure make you *so* comfortable that you forget either your good manners or business and professional ethics. You have asked the person across the desk for his or her time and thoughtful answers. Even if you think you see an opening for a real job, don't even hint at it. For one thing, you're really not *ready* for an employment interview yet; you're still gathering information. For another, the person you're interviewing may feel you got this appointment under false pretenses, and feel justifiably upset or angry or both. In any case, such a response from someone employed in a field that interests you can't do you any good later on.

How do you locate potential interviewees? Through your personal network. Though you may not have used it extensively, you *do have* a network. Your family, relatives, friends, and neighbors are all a part of it, of course. But, also think of all the people you know — even casually — and those you do business with. Professors, clergy, doctors, dentists, insurance agents, lawyers — and just about anyone you wrote a check to during the past year. And, don't forget your classmates and *their* friends and relatives. They're all part of your personal network.

One set will be "warm contacts" — people with whom you have some connection. Those you have no connection with are "cold" contacts. Warm contacts may include near-peers — perhaps a friend who graduated a year or two back who's now working in a career that interests you. Warm contacts can also include the parents of your college friends, and both friends and associates of your parents, relatives, and other friends. In short, warm contacts probably know you or know of you.

Before you write the older members of this group asking for an interview, you might ask the person you know mutually to informally inquire if the contact would be welcomed. *That's* a communication that can be handled in person — perhaps over lunch or at a business meeting — or by phone. Your first communication with the potential contact should be a brief letter requesting their time in a short meeting.

"Cold" contacts are people you don't know. You may get their names from business directories or people who know them. Because these interviews may not be quite as comfortable as those with your warm contacts, it's probably a good idea to start with the latter.

Your letter requesting the interview should only be three or four paragraphs in length. Begin by telling who you are, where you're in school, when you'll graduate, why you're interested in their career field, that you're presently gathering information on that field, and that you'd appreciate a few minutes of their time to learn more about the career and what it's like to be in it. Make your tone friendly, but businesslike. Remember, you're likely asking a busy professional to take time out of a day to do you a favor. You might even want to acknowledge this in the letter itself. Then, close with something like, "I'd like to phone you on (day and date) to ask when it might be convenient to see me briefly."

Then, be certain to follow up with that phone call on the day you suggested. Business people appreciate consistency and being able to count on someone to do what they say they'll do. When you speak to your contact, make it clear that you only want 20 or 30 minutes of their time. When they confirm the appointment, repeat the day, date and time — "Fine, that's Thursday, the eighth, at 9:30 a.m. I look forward to seeing you then."

Before you go, though, make sure you do some more "homework." There is a lot of information you can get about a person's business and their career from sources mentioned in the previous chapter. Don't take their time asking questions you could (and should) have answered before your meeting. They'll appreciate your preparation, and you'll be much more comfortable in the interview.

After you've done your research, make a list of questions you either could not answer through other material — or, perhaps, information you'd like your contact to confirm and/or expand on. Actually write out your questions. And, consider leaving room between them to note your answers during the interview.

Here are some thought-starters:

What interested you in this career? Why do you believe it's a good career choice?

If you were choosing a career today, would you make the same choice?

What is most satisfying about your career? Do you enjoy coming to work every day?

Would you recommend that your son or daughter follow in your footsteps?

What are the most important qualifications to succeed in it?

What is your typical day like?

What do you like most about this field? What do you like least?

What was your biggest success? Your biggest disappointment?

What are the big issues in your field today?

What are the major problems? Opportunities?

How has your field changed since you entered it?

How secure is this field today? Is it growing or shrinking?

How rapidly can someone expect to advance in this career?

What can one expect to be doing and earning in two years? In five?

How much competition is there among your peers?

If you could give me one solid piece of advice, what would it be?

Is there anything else I should have asked, but didn't?

Before you conclude the conversation, be sure to ask if your contact can suggest other people you should talk with. You'll be expanding your personal network geometrically, and someone who is active and successful in a career is the best source for introductions to other people like them.

If your interview goes well and your contact doesn't seem to be in a hurry to end it, consider asking if you might have a brief tour of the office or work area. This will give you the opportunity to "pick up some vibes" of what it's actually like to work in this field. You'll also gain some valuable first-hand impressions of actual businesses which employ people in that career. This may be very helpful later on when you're deciding whom to approach for an employment interview.

After each interview, be sure to write your contact a note of appreciation for his or her time and thoughtful answers. If a friend or relative helped set up the contact, a note or phone call confirming that you have held the interview is appropriate.

Don't stop with one or two informational interviews in each field that interests you. By talking with a number of people, some trends will emerge — and you will be closer still to making your decision based on solid information and the "feelings" you get from those you interview.

Write a brief summary of the experience after each interview. A 5 x 7 card is a good place to make these notes. You can file them for later reference when you want to recall how a place "felt" and impressions you gained while you were there. Cross-referencing these cards with your notes from the interview is a good idea, too.

The informational interview is an excellent "fact finding" strategy. It puts you face-to-face with people who are making a career in a field that interests you. You'll gain valuable insights into how these people react to their world of work...and how that world is treating them. You may not care for all the people you interview. Some you may "take to" instantly and even strike up a friendship.

But, if you come up against a full dozen people in the same field who are cranky and dissatisfied with their lot in life, you will have received a strong message that it might make sense to shift gears and consider another field. On the other hand, one or two of those you interview for informational purposes could even become your mentors.

Your personal network is a powerful tool that can help put you in touch with people who can give you good, solid information about your potential career field — through the informational interview — and people who can *also* put you in touch with still other people who can help you in your job search.

Using private employment agencies
Employment agencies can be a useful part of your job search, but it's important to understand how they work, how they can help you, and how to use them to your own best advantage. The section which follows concerns only private employment agencies, not executive search firms — which usually only work with managers and other very experienced employees.

If you *do* choose to contact an employment agency, *do not* turn your job search over to this or any other third party. Use them only as a supplement to your own activities. Experts in the employment field recommend that you only devote about ten percent of your search time to working with an agency.

It is estimated that there are probably eight to ten thousand private employment agencies in the U.S. today. Many agencies specialize in certain industries — banking, accounting, data processing, medical services, or engineering, for example — and often prefer to work only with experienced applicants. Other agencies place clerical workers and secretaries. But, some agencies do specialize in working with recent college graduates.

Here are some insights into how agencies work and how you can work with one to your own best advantage:

Nearly all sizeable companies work with employment agencies; many become closely allied with one or two agencies and give them most of their business.

Agencies are not usually "retained" by an employer — they work on a contingency basis. If they don't fill a job opening, they don't get paid.

Most agencies today also work on a "fee paid" basis — meaning the employer pays their fee for filling a job. You should try to negotiate this arrangement.

However, some agencies still look to the job seeker for their commission — a hefty percentage of the person's first year's salary. Were you to contract with such an agency, they may legally require you to pay their fee even if you quit the new job a few weeks after taking it.

If an agency asks you to sign any form, read it very carefully. It may be a contract requiring you to pay for their services. If you agree to do this, ask how long you must keep a job before you are obligated to pay their fee — and get their answer in writing.

Do not sign an agreement to work with any agency exclusively. Some who do wind up paying the agency for a job they got for themselves. Again, read any agreements carefully, and don't sign anything that you don't understand or has questionable language.

Remember that an employer who hires you through an agency is likely paying more for your services than had you been hired on the "open market." This means that the agency may be getting some of your first year's income whether or not you pay them directly.

Agencies can work against you by calling firms you've already contacted — and trying to place other candidates they represent. So be wary about saying much about your own job search.

Ask people in your network to recommend agencies with which they've had a good experience. When you get a firm's name, ask your contact for the name of the recruiter he or she worked with.

It's best to make your initial contact with an agency in person. After setting up an interview with a particular recruiter by phone, go there. As he or she is interviewing you, you can also interview the recruiter. Find out how long the person has been with the agency and in the agency field. Check out the offices and find out about their standards. Is it a quality operation? Are these the kind of people you feel you can work with comfortably? Do you believe they will represent you well? How much pressure do you feel in the initial interview? If they're pressuring you, chances are they're doing the same thing with employers.

Remember, you are free to say "no" to an interview or a job offer. And, if you don't like the way the agency is handling their part of your search, you can decide not to work with them further.

There are two types of agencies — permanent and temporary. Sometimes they are two divisions of the same firm. And you may consider registering with both of them. "Temping" can give you some income while you continue your search for a permanent position, and the experience will give you a good, inside look at a number of companies. Also, you may receive an offer of permanent employment if a company likes what you do for them as a "temp."

Insist that the agency check with you before sending your resumé to a prospective employer; you don't want them duplicating your own efforts.

Employment agencies do know where current openings are, and they can get you interviews. However, even if you're working with an agency, you should not abdicate to them or any other entity your responsibility for finding a position.

If you do decide to work with an agency, check with them regularly. They can give you feedback from interviews they arrange. And, through regular contact, you can determine what they're doing in your behalf. It's your job search, remember. And you may find it necessary to be assertive with the agency to maintain control of that search and to use them to your own best advantage.

Answering ads

Big city newspapers often have pages of ads for job openings. Small town papers will have fewer ads, but they should be checked regularly. Ads will also appear in association newsletters and trade publications. Other job sources include:

- Business newspapers

- School/university job postings

- Bulletin boards in community centers

- Government publications

However, the director of a major midwestern university's career office says that the major daily in his area will usually carry ads for fewer than ten percent of the local jobs available at any given time. So *use* the newspaper and these other sources, but don't rely on them too heavily. They should never be your sole — or even major — source for employment leads.

There are two types of job ads:

Open ads list the company's name, usually with address and phone number and a name to contact. After responding to these ads, you can follow up by phone to determine whether your letter and resumé were received...and possibly even get the employer's reaction to them.

Blind ads are "lower yield" than open ads. They don't reveal the company name, and the reply address will often be a post office box number. Companies publish blind ads for several reasons.

The company doesn't want to respond to every candidate; that takes time and money. And they don't want to be inundated by job seekers following up on their applications by phone.

They don't want the public or present employees to know that some key personnel change is about to occur.

There may not be a current job opening at all. The ad may have been placed by an employment agency seeking to stockpile resumés to use when the next real opening does occur.

Which ads should you respond to? Even if you don't have *all* the qualifications for a position that interests you, respond anyway. Ads often describe the "ideal candidate" which companies rarely find. Also, look for companies that run large ads listing many openings. Even if your qualifications aren't exactly right for a listed position, there may be other current or future openings for which you would be an excellent candidate.

How to answer an ad? Those that include a phone number *expect* a call. It will often be an employment agency. If you have the choice between calling and writing, call. You'll have the opportunity to establish some rapport over the phone and learn more precisely what the interviewer is looking for.

When you call, have your notes handy which outline your strengths as they apply to that position. This will help you speak quickly and clearly about yourself. And don't be hesitant to ask questions — your concerns are important. You don't want to waste your time interviewing for a position that doesn't really suit you.

Blind ads, of course, require a written response. But even some which list a company's name may only receive applications by mail. However, if you do know the company's name, some of your contacts may be able to help you "network" your way into the firm for an interview.

Here are some tips for responding to an ad:
Before writing a letter or making a phone call, you need to do a little more homework.

First, identify the key assets or traits the advertiser seems to be seeking. Write them out and underline key words.

List your own assets, experience, or traits that match those in the ad.

Try to work these into a "double table" of needs and assets. This can become a critical part of your phone response — or a key to your written follow-up.

If you're writing, make the rest of your letter short and sweet. If it's appropriate, you can refer to your attached resumé.

Try to avoid the issue of salary requirements — reserving this, hopefully, for an interview.

Here are two sample letters for following up on a newspaper ad. The first is a response to an "open" ad:

Michael Dillon
103 East 90th Street
New York, NY 10028

June 21, 1993

Mr. William Johnson
Manufacturing Manager
DONCO Products, Inc.
123 Main Street
White Plains, NY 13480

Dear Mr. Johnson:

I am responding to your recent advertisement for a Marketing Trainee at DONCO Products. I believe my strong background in direct selling may be of great value to you.

While working on my bachelor's degree in business at NYU, my experience includes two summers of varied line production work and two other summers selling consumer products in a retail outlet. In addition, I often acted as assistant store manager in times of peak sales volumes, especially during holiday periods.

I have been successful in several areas I think will be of interest to a growing firm like DONCO Products. In particular, I have:

- Increased sales significantly for a long-term obsolescent product; and,

- Assisted in motivating a part-time sales staff during busy holiday periods.

I am enclosing a copy of my resumé for your review. I look forward to hearing from you soon. You may reach me by mail at the above address, or by phone at (212) 555-3131.

Sincerely,

Michael Dillon

And, this is a typical response to a "blind" ad:

Dorothy Conlin
61 Perry Street
New York, NY 10014
(212) 555-2121

June 21, 1993

F5861
New York Times
New York, NY 10108

Dear Sir or Madam:

I am writing in response to your advertisement for a Customer Service Administrator.

For the past two years I have been employed part-time in the Customer Service Department of the D-J Textile Company while completing my degree in marketing at City College. My duties at D-J Textile included working at a CRT terminal, taking over-the-phone purchase orders, and responding to customer complaints — making adjustments to their accounts as necessary.

I am enclosing my resumé for your information. I look forward to receiving your reply in the near future.

Very truly yours,

Dorothy Conlin

Networking, informational interviewing, perhaps using employment agencies, and responding to ads in newspapers and other publications: they are all useful strategies in a thorough, well-organized, and successful job search. None of them is sufficient. However, used together — even synergistically — they can help move you from student to interviewee and potential employee. To move beyond this point, you'll need to do just a bit more "homework" — perfecting your resumé, cover letters, and both interviewing and negotiating skills for your first career position after college.

Making contact

Your resumé

This is an essential document — a combination of pedigree, dossier, press release, promotional device, and key marketing tool. *Do not underestimate the importance of a good, effective resumé.* At the same time, don't expect it to obtain a job for you. The most you can expect of a good resumé and an effective cover letter is that they will sufficiently interest a potential employer (or, most likely, a recruiter or applicant "screener" for that employer) to pass these documents on to someone who can invite you to interview for a position.

You need to be aware that the first responsibility among people who screen resumés is to find reasons to eliminate job seekers from further consideration. *Your* first responsibility in constructing your resumé is simple — don't give them any reasons.

For those jobs that require good written communication skills, your resumé and the cover letter that accompanies it can be great showcases of your talents. When you send your resumé to a prospective employer, it is "you" — on paper. As such, it is just as important in creating a good first impression as over-the-phone or face-to-face contacts are. If you have succeeded in gaining an interview without sending your resumé ahead of you — perhaps through the personal recommendation of a network contact — your resumé is a good "leave-behind" piece to remind the employer of you after the interview.

The resumé is a distilled and organized compilation of your education, selected experiences and achievements, and your skills and abilities. Properly ordered, these elements should translate what you have done in the past to what you can do in the future for an employer. Reading it, the employer (or his or her representative) should easily be able to discern:

• Who you are

• The type of work you seek

• What you know

• What you have learned and done

• What you are capable of doing

A successful resumé will project something of your own spirit and uniqueness. It will also speak to the needs and interests of the employer — focusing on skills and abilities that are important to his needs and experiences that are relevant to his available position.

The first thing resumé readers usually notice is the overall appearance of the document. If it's sloppy, overly crowded or full of errors, there's an excellent chance they won't even read it. Such a document presents you in a very negative light. Here's a quick checklist to help ensure that you make a good first impression on paper.

Your resumé should be:
Neat and clean with ample margins on top, bottom and sides.

Easy to read. The print size should be at least 10 point for eye comfort. Bold and underlined matter should enhance readability, but never be overdone.

Flawless — with no spelling errors or typos.

No more than two pages — a single page is preferred for entry-level job candidates.

Written on a word processor if at all possible — the appearance is much more professional than can be achieved using a typewriter.

Printed on high quality bond or laser printer paper.

On the same quality and color paper as your cover letter.

Your own work. Don't let anyone else write your resumé. You know you best.

Think about your resumé as a living thing that can grow to reflect your own development. You may want to compose a resumé early in your job search just in case a "real" offer comes along during your preparation phase. However, as you gain knowledge of the career or industry you've targeted, update your resumé to reflect your greater knowledge. For example, you may find that entry-level opportunities for advertising media buyers are soft, but that openings for media planners and analysts are wide open right now. If you have any experience in planning and analysis, you'll want to revise your resumé to reflect this new interest and direction.

Also, because you will want to refine your resumé as your job search progresses, it's probably best not to have 500 copies printed. Start with 15 or 20 copies photocopied onto good quality white or light cream bond paper. Bond has a cotton rag content that makes the paper crisp. A 16 to 20 pound weight is appropriate; anything heavier may appear to be extravagant. Don't use erasable bond or colored stock — other than a light cream. You'll be approaching business and professional people who don't usually correspond on colored paper. You want your resumé to stand out — but for the *right* reasons.

While it is true that your resumé should have a format, content, and appearance that accurately reflects your individuality, it should also follow some general guidelines. By adhering to these guidelines, you'll be able to present yourself in the best possible light.

Resumé formats

Although resumés come in several formats, the two types most widely used are:

The chronological resumé, which lists various jobs in reverse order, the latest first. It usually includes a description of each job and a list of the writer's accomplishments in each position.

The functional resumé avoids, or plays down, the employment record. It emphasizes your experience and accomplishments in each functional area — particularly the one(s) in which you seek employment. This allows the writer to downplay certain work experiences and highlight others. The functional resumé also provides the best format for emphasizing accomplishments outside of formal employment situations — such as experience gained in volunteer work, in school, and through hobbies.

Both forms will be improved by listing accomplishments in each job or function.

The functional resumé, however, describes your work experience and accomplishments in terms of functions. If, for example, you demonstrated the ability to plan and organize a community event, you could easily display that skill and supporting documentation in the functional resumé. It gives you more flexibility to highlight various work areas.

Examples of both types of resumés are included at the end of this chapter.

Objective and summary statements

As most resumés are read by busy people, it's to your advantage to get your key message across in a quick, interesting way very early.

The first thing most resumé readers want to know is: "What kind of position are you looking for?" One way to answer this question is to begin the resumé with a description of your objective. Examples:

A copyrighting, editing, or general advertising position within an agency or corporate department.

A technical training position which will take advantage of my three years' experience in summer jobs.

A marketing training position in the sales division of a small to medium-size company.

Many graduates have more than one objective and, therefore, would accept more than one type of job offer. If this is the case, it's best to tailor separate resumés to fit each objective. Or, you may prefer to leave the objective statement out of the resumé and include it in your cover letter.

Because most employers also want to know what kind of job candidate you are and what you can actually *do*, a summary statement (following your objective statement if placed in your resumé) can answer this question. A summary statement presents the broad picture of who you are and what an employer can expect from you. Some resumé readers won't bother reading further if the document has no summary statement — it saves them time and speeds their judgment process. The objective statement and summary statement *must* always be in agreement. Examples:

Objective statement in cover letter	**Summary statement in resumé**
An accounting position with a Big Six firm in the Northeast.	An organized, detail-oriented business school graduate with accounting major and summer experience in mid-size NYC firms. Solid accomplishments in cost accounting and budget planning. Works well under pressure.
A laboratory position with a bio-engineering firm in California.	An energetic, highly motivated Master's graduate in biochemistry with four years' experience as laboratory assistant manager. Graduate fellowship with National Academy of Sciences.

61

| An environmental engineer in an international organization. | A results-oriented engineering graduate with a minor in environmental studies; worked for three summers with Jacques Cousteau. |

Education

Most recent graduates' work experience consists of several summer jobs which lasted only a few months and required rather basic skills. Because these experiences aren't the major thing they have to "sell" a prospective employer, many choose to put their Education section before their Experience section in the resumé.

List your educational history in a reverse chronology — beginning with your latest (or anticipated) degree first. Include experiences you've had during your education that corroborate your ability to fulfill the position you are applying for. If you did a substantial research project, describe it. If you have taken courses that support your job ambitions, but are not a part of your major, specify what you learned and how it will contribute to your competency on the job. If you speak and/or write a language other than English, say so and specify your level of competence. If you are skilled in the use of a computer or word processor, include this information — along with the programs you have mastered.

If you acquired a Grade Point Average of 3.2 or better, include this in the Education section of your resumé. If your overall average wasn't that great — but was much better, for example, in your senior year — indicate this. Some employers, notably financial institutions and consulting firms, insist on seeing a GPA before they will seriously consider a candidate.

If you attended a college or university other than the one from which you graduated, list this school second in your Education section. Include any special honors, courses, or experiences which relate to your career goal. Extracurricular, public service, and volunteer activities are important and should be included. They portray the breadth of your interests and demonstrate that you were not in school either just to study...or to play. Fraternity, sorority, and club memberships can be included in your Education section or, if they are numerous, in a separate Activities section. But emphasize your leadership positions under Experience.

Experience
This section relates the positions you have held and both your responsibilities and accomplishments during each tenure. Use action verbs (created, led, organized, presented, etc.) to describe your activities and achievements as dynamically as possible. Include all your positions — including volunteer, part-time, internships, and work-study positions.

Do not include
Any mention of your age, race, religion, gender, national origin, marital status, or number of children. This information is not work-related, but could be used to screen you out. The courts have ruled this information may be the basis for discrimination, and is therefore illegal for an employer to ask. Why offer it?

Your physical description or mention of your height, weight, or general health.

Any listing of references — or even a mention. It's assumed that most people seeking a job have people who will recommend them. Wait until you're asked for your references.

Any reference to salary earned in earlier positions or salary requirements for the job sought.

Do not include the word "resumé" at the top of the document. Almost everyone knows what one looks like.

Resumés and cover letters
Your first objective, of course, is a face-to-face meeting with the interviewer or contact. From this perspective, sending the resumé is a compromise. It's "you" — only not

in person. Also, as it's a standardized document, it can't be an exact match for every situation. When asked for your resumé, always send a well-written and tailor-made cover letter with it. The cover letter becomes your customizing tool — introducing your resumé with a particular focus, addressing your job objectives and, if known, the specific needs of the reader. Highlight your relevant educational and work experiences to help the reader recognize the the position in his or her organization.

Writing the resumé

Armed with the advice on the preceding pages, you can now write your resumé. Use the exercise sheets provided on the following pages to develop a chronological resumé first, then — if you wish — use that to construct the one with a functional format.

Don't get discouraged if you don't create a masterpiece right away. It may well take you several drafts before you have a document you're comfortable with — a resumé that creates as accurate and positive an impression of you as possible.

Remember, the resumé is only a tool in your job search. But, it is a vital tool. You'll be presenting it to prospective employers, personnel counselors, and various contacts you'll meet in your job-hunting process. To be most useful to you, you have to feel good about your resumé. If you're not satisfied with your early results, keep working. Get advice from someone you respect. If you're still at your college or university, ask a professional in your career office for advice and critique. You should be pleased with the resumé you come up with as your final product. If it's "right" for you, you'll be proud to present it as your personal advertisement.

Chronological Resumé Format

_____Name
_____Address
_____City, State, Zip
_____Telephone Number

POSITION OBJECTIVE

_____
_____

BACKGROUND SUMMARY

_____
_____

EDUCATION

School_____
Location (City, State)_____
Year of Graduation_____
Degree and Major Field_____
GPA, Activities, Organizations_____

WORK EXPERIENCE

Company_____Location (City, State)_____
Dates Employed_____Job Title_____
Responsibilities:_____

Accomplishments:_____
_____
_____
_____

Company_____Location (City, State)_____
Dates Employed_____Job Title_____
Responsibilities:_____

Accomplishments:_____
_____
_____
_____

Company_____Location (City, State)_____
Dates Employed_____Job Title_____
Responsibilities:_____

Accomplishments:_____
_____
_____
_____

Functional Resumé Format

_____Name
_____Address
_____City, State, Zip
_____Telephone Number

POSITION OBJECTIVE

_____
_____

BACKGROUND SUMMARY

_____
_____

MAJOR ACCOMPLISHMENTS
_____(Function)

_____
_____
_____

_____(Function)

_____
_____
_____

EDUCATION
School_____Location (City, State)_____
Year of Graduation_____
Degree and Major Field_____
GPA, Activities, Organizations_____

WORK EXPERIENCE

Company_____Location (City, State)_____
Dates Employed_____Job Title_____
Responsibilities:_____
Accomplishments:_____
_____
_____

Company_____Location (City, State)_____
Dates Employed_____Job Title_____
Responsibilities:_____
Accomplishments:_____
_____
_____

Company_____Location (City, State)_____
Dates Employed_____Job Title_____
Responsibilities:_____
Accomplishments:_____
_____
_____

Beth A. Owens
196 Prospect Street
Madison, NJ 07940
(201) 721-8702

Professional Objective
An entry-level position in international banking

Education
Colgate University, B.A., 1993. Concentration in international relations/political science. 3.4 GPA (4-point scale). Additional courses in computer sciences, French, and Spanish.

University of Hartford, summer 1993. Graduate-level courses in marketing, corporate finance, intermediate accounting, and federal taxation.

Honors
Graduated Cum Laude from Colgate University.
Dean's List six out of eight semesters.
Phi Eta Sigma, Freshman Honor Society.
Pi Sigma Alpha, National Political Science Honor Society.
Selected Member, Geneva Study Group. Intensive study in European politics, organizations, banking, and trade relations. Fall 1991.

Experience
Research Assistant, Psychology Department, Colgate University. Assisted in coding and analyzing data from various studies. Results pending publication. Winter 1992-1993.

Bank Teller, Midlantic North Bank, West Paterson, NJ. Managed and processed financial transactions. Gained knowledge of banking procedures. Summer 1992.

Manager (Part-time), Village Shop, a women's clothing store, Wayne, NJ. Supervised employees, managed daily financial transactions, and developed public relations skills. Summers, school holidays, 1988-1991.

Waitress/Hostess, Oliver's Restaurant, Yarmouth, MA. Developed public relations skills. Facilitated the flow of business and handled customer complaints. Summer 1987.

Co-Curricular Activities

Writer, The Colgate News. Researched and wrote feature articles as well as regular sports coverage.

Dorm Representative, West Hall Dormitory, Colgate University. Organized various student activities.

Martha A. Evans
241 Huntington Street
Brentwood, NY 11717
(516) 838-7409

Objective: Seeking a position in computer programming with opportunities for advancement in systems analysis.

Education: Monmouth College, West Long Branch, NJ 07764
Course of study: Computer Science
Projected Graduation: May 1993
Overall GPA 3.7; GPA in Major 3.8

Experience: Employed during Spring and Fall Intercessions through the following agencies:

1991 to present
Data Entry Temporaries, Parsippany, NJ
Companies included:
Warner Lambert, BASF
Responsibilities included:
    Data entry, general clerical skills

1990 to present
Hartshorn Services, Parsippany, NJ
Companies included:
Hertz, Citicorp, Metem Corporation,
Daily Record
Responsibilities included:
    Receptionist, general clerical skills

1989 to present
Office Force, Cedar Knolls, NJ
Companies included:
Fireman's Fund Insurance Co.,
Office Force
Responsibilities included:
    Data entry, general clerical skills, entrusted with running the office for Office Force during their relocation to New Jersey

Specialized Skills:

Software	**Hardware**
PASCAL, COBOL, GW BASIC, C	BTI,
IBM 360/370 Assembler	Perkin-Elmer 3250XP
Rockwell R6502 Microprocessor	AIM 65 Microcomputer
VI Editor	AT&T PC

Activities:
President, Computer Science Honor Society, 1991-present.
Member, Computer Science Honor Society, 1990.
Member, Mathematics Honor Society, 1991-present.
Member, Monmouth College Honors Program, 1989-present.
Member, Gamma Sigma National Service Sorority, 1989-1992.

Functional Model Resumé

Raymond F. Adriance
2912 West Jefferson Street
Summit, CO 80221
Home: (303) 106-7122
Office: (303) 121-0067

Job Goal: Professional or management position in training function of a growth-oriented organization.

Summary: As training assistant, coordinated the development and delivery of company management and supervisory development programs.

Major Accomplishments: Research and Needs Analysis
Developed management audit to assess strengths and training deficits of supervisory and management personnel. Designed data collection system to utilize current computer capabilities in company. Assessed long-range manpower requirements resulting in allocation of $750,000 additional funding for recruitment, hiring, and training.

Program Design, Development, and Delivery
Coordinated development of customized training programs using in-house staff.

Trained over 60 managers in "How to Manage More Effectively."

Chosen as keynote speaker for area conference on Training and Development.

Supervision and Administration
Supervised seven professional staff and three support persons.

Developed and monitored $1,000,000 training budget.

Effectively recruited and trained five new program specialists.

Work History:

1991-Present   Coordinator, Human Resources, Allstate Bank, Littleton, CO

1988-1991   Administrative Assistant, Littleton Chamber of Commerce, Littleton, CO

1985-1988   Military Service, Honorable Discharge

Education: University of Colorado at Denver, Bachelor of Science in Business Administration, Anticipated Graduation: May 1993

Related Professional

Experience: Member, Rocky Mountain Chapter, American Society for Training and Development

Resumé checklist

1. Is it readable with varied use of short paragraphs, bullets, and white space?

2. Is it interesting? Would you want to read it if you were the prospective employer?

3. Is it clear? Would an employer know within one minute what type of job you want and why you were qualified?

4. Is it professional? Is it "letter perfect" with no misspellings, typos, or fingerprints?

5. Is it comprehensive without being exhaustive?

6. Have you quantified some of your accomplishments?

7. Is it accurate and honest?

8. Does it "invite" the reader to find out more about you?

9. Did you use action verbs to describe accomplishments?

10. Do your accomplishment statements support your stated job objective?

11. When you read over your resumé, are *you* impressed? Do you feel a sense of pride and accomplishment?

12. Would *you* hire you?

Cover letters

By definition, cover letters are brief communications that accompany your resumé when you mail it. What you write in your letter depends on the reason you're sending your resumé.

A good cover letter:

- Uses a standard business format and employs a business/professional tone

- Is written to an individual if possible, not to a function or to "Dear Sir or Madam"

- Is written on the same paper stock (and color) as your resumé (if possible)

- Is just as neat, visually attractive, and error-free as your resumé

- Includes your telephone number (it may get separated from your resumé)

- Is four or five paragraphs in length — written on a single page

- Tells the recipient why you are writing (response to an ad, referral by a mutual friend, etc.)

- Specifies the position (or type of position) you are interested in filling

- Speaks to the needs and interests of the reader; demonstrates that your education, abilities, and interests are relevant to his or her job opening

- Lets the reader know that you know something about his or her company, that you've gone to the trouble of doing some research before writing

- States your key skills and abilities

- Should always be individually typed or written on a word processor with a letter quality printer; never send a photocopy of a generic cover letter

- Has a conversational tone, but does not presume a friendship with the reader

- States how you would like the recipient to respond or states that you will follow up by telephone on a specified date or during a certain week

- Requests an interview

- Thanks the reader

- Closes with "Sincerely" or "Yours truly" — "Cordially" may seem presumptuous

Sample Cover Letter "A"

Margaret Greenacre
1001 Long Street
Marietta, GA 30068
(404) 928-3882

(Date)

Ms. Marion W. Crane
Vice President
First National Bank
100 Main Street
Knoxville, TN 37902

Dear Ms. Crane:

A friend of my parents, Joan Cooper in your Commercial
Lending Department, recently told me the bank may be seeking
a marketing assistant. As you can see from my resumé, I am
about to complete my B.S. degree in business administration
with a concentration in marketing at Georgia State University.
I have attended GSU in the evenings while working full time at
Trust Company Bank in Atlanta.

Some of my present responsibilities include:

• Overseeing the services provided by an outside public relations
  firm

• Coordinating the gathering of demographic data on present
  customers

• Supervising a staff of clerical assistants

I would very much like to meet with you to discuss your open
position. If I may, I will phone you next Tuesday, the 12th,
to ask if I might meet with you for an interview. Should you
want to reach me before then, please phone me at home at
(404) 928-3882.

Sincerely,

Margaret Greenacre

Sample Cover Letter "B"

Diana Browning
92 West Davis Street
Pittsburgh, PA 32618

(Date)

Dr. William L. Green, Director
Medical Testing Department
L. L. Magers Medical Center
122 Evergreen Drive
Bethlehem, PA 18515

Dear Dr. Green:

I am writing in response to your ad in the Pittsburgh <u>Dispatch</u>
for a Coordinator of Medical Assistants. As you requested, I am
enclosing a resumé summarizing my education, qualifications,
and work experience.

In line with your advertisement, my summer and part-time work
experience includes:

- Exercise testing

- Blood pressure monitoring

- Coordinating activities of medical assistants

I am graduating from the University of Pittsburgh in June and
plan to move to the Lehigh Valley area about the first of July. I
would like very much to meet you to discuss employment opportunities with your medical center.

I will be in touch with your office by phone next week. However,
if you should want to reach me before that time, please phone
me at (315) 928-6250.

Thank you for your consideration.

Sincerely,

Diana Browning

The on-campus interview

These interviews differ from those conducted in a company's offices in several important ways:

As most campus interviews last only 30 minutes, there is significant time pressure on the interviewer.

The home office interview centers around the question "to hire or not to hire?" The campus interview is much more of an information-gathering exercise in which the interviewer's principal responsibility is to identify and quantify the most attractive job candidates.

Because he or she may already have interviewed a number of candidates, the interviewer may not be well-focused on your discussion; fatigue and boredom can be a problem for both of you.

Unlike the home office interview, the interviewer knows he or she must also "sell" the company to interviewees.

The campus interview model
A model for the campus interview has been constructed by industry to minimize the impact of three realities listed above: time pressure, fatigue and boredom, and the need to sell. This model has been widely used by a number of major corporations and has been found to work well in most on-campus situations. Knowing the other side's strategy is always a major factor in "winning." If he or she

is following the widely accepted model, the interviewer's strategy looks like this:

I	Opening comments
II	Specific facts
III	Broad-brush questions
IV	Applicant's job wants
V	Sell the company
VI	Applicant's questions
VII	Next steps

Here is a point-for-point analysis of this interview model — using our knowledge of the constraints, demands, and pressures on the interviewer to provide insights that should prove helpful to you in this interview situation.

Opening comments

Because time is at a premium, the interviewer will likely devote only three to five minutes establishing rapport with you. And, you may find to your absolute delight that *you* are more at ease than your interviewer. After all, this *is* your turf! Interviewers will, of course, feel the need to "control" the situation. However, they realize they cannot dominate the discussion. He or she also wants to hear from you and learn more about the type of person you are and the things that are important to you in a career position. During these opening moments, you may hear your interviewer say something like:

> "I know that in our meeting today we are both attempting to learn a little about what we can offer each other. I certainly would like to learn about your background and interests. And I know you are interested in learning about what our company has to offer. So, let's divide up the time a bit. I'd like to spend the first half of the interview getting acquainted with you, then we'll turn it around and you can learn more about us. Okay?"

Specific facts

Most organizations which conduct campus interviews insist that their representatives gather certain specific information about job candidates. To avoid running out of time and failing to get this data by waiting until near the end of the interview, early on you can expect to be asked at least four things:

To sign a transcript request for the release of your academic records

Whether the address and phone number on your resumé are correct and current

Whether you expect to graduate in June (or at the end of the present quarter or semester)

Whether you have had contact with other personnel of the company the interviewer represents.

Some companies send several interviewers to the same campus on the same day. They don't want to duplicate their associates' efforts, nor do they want to have their people sending you multiples of the same interview follow-up letter. (If several different divisions of the same firm are on campus, there is also the issue of your receiving invitations for further interviews from one group and turndowns from others.)

Broad-brush questions
These are basically open-ended questions designed to make you "think on your feet." By doing this, the interviewer seeks to make certain observations about your behavior, how you think, your poise, and your general personal characteristics. You'll probably get two or three broad-brush questions such as:

"What long-term satisfaction do you expect to derive from a career in ___?"

"How do you evaluate a college career as preparation for the future?"

"What are your thoughts about how (accounting, writing, etc.) will sustain your interest and motivation in the years ahead?"

In listening to you, you may find that the interviewer is "accepting the applicant" (you) through comments that encourage you to speak out and elaborate — "uh-huh," "go on," "I understand," and "that's interesting." Interviewers are taught that such comments encourage conversation without either condemning or condoning what is being said.

You'll also likely hear your interviewer "restate and reflect" your words. He or she listens, then "mirrors" what you said through other words. The theory is that people will reveal even more information about themselves when they feel accepted and understood.

Be alert for a pause or silence in the interviewer's part of the dialogue. This is said to be "one of the most powerful tools in an interviewer's repertoire." When a pause occurs during a discussion, there is tremendous psychological pressure to fill the conversational void. And most of the pressure will be on you, not the interviewer. He or she may intentionally create a silence just to see whether you "jump" to fill it...and, if you do, what you fill it *with*! If you are the one who pauses, let it be clear that you do so because you're thinking. But, again, don't be so eager to end the silence that you wind up saying something you may later regret.

Applicant's job wants and selling the company

This part of your discussion often combines steps IV and V of the interview model. By finding out what's important to you in a job, the savvy interviewer will also know how best to "sell" the company to you. Your best strategy at this juncture is to be honest in relating what really *is* important to you in an anticipated employment situation, then listen carefully to whether — and how — your interviewer matches your concerns with either realities or promises about his or her firm.

Applicant's questions

After proceeding through steps IV and V above, the interviewer will want to entertain any questions you may have. The very nature of those questions will provide definite clues for him or her to assess your desires, motivations, and additional avenues which might successfully sell you on the company.

Interviewers are encouraged to be frank and honest in responding to your questions. If you ask something to which he or she has no answer, the response should be, "I don't know, but I'll find out for you." Hearing this is a good indication that the interviewer is "shooting straight" with you on other important points.

Next steps

In many cases, campus interviewers will indicate that you should hear something from the company in about two weeks. However, you shouldn't expect the interviewer to indicate what that communication will be. Interviewers don't want to commit their companies to additional interviews or company visits until they have had the opportunity to review their notes on all interviewees. If you aren't issued an invitation here, don't be discouraged. It may be just too early for one.

Now that you've had a look at the campus interview from the perspective of the other side of the table, perhaps you'll be more relaxed and better able to enjoy these experiences. Good luck!

Interviewing in the marketplace

A perspective on the interview
Some people believe the job interview is the only way to get a job. However, as you know by now, the interview is actually only a part of the effort. While it *is* usually an essential element in the search for a position, it is really only the culmination of a lot of other activities.

If you think like a marketer, the job interview is an important selling event that follows a lot of hard work in market research, strategic planning, marketing communications, and other elements of your marketing campaign. The interview is your final marketing event — the last hurdle between you and a job offer. As such, it is well worth your time to prepare for this occasion.

Drake Beam Morin's wide experience over more than 25 years indicates that it usually takes about five interviews to get one job offer. The ideal search yields two or three offers before the "right match" is achieved. Remember, this is your choice as well as the employer's. Your first offer may be a perfect "fit" and you may accept it, but it is unlikely that the job interview will be a one-time event in your search. Others will want to meet you and you will want to meet them so you can compare companies. And, while those meetings may not be actual "hiring" interviews, they are interviews nonetheless. So, building strong interview skills can help you through a successful job search and into your new job as well.

This chapter will help you prepare for your interviews in many ways — from conducting company research and dressing for the occasion to communicating confidence during the interview itself. Your self-confidence is essential to a successful interview. And all the following information is geared to helping you build confidence in yourself and your ability to perform well in the interview situation.

There are two types of job interviews: the screening interview and the decision interview. Each type is conducted by a different kind of interviewer, and for a different purpose.

Screening interviews
These are usually given by:
Employment agency representatives

• Usually experienced interviewers (unless they are recently hired)

• Who would like to "package and sell" you quickly (because they work on commission)

• Who may sacrifice your wants to place you quickly

• Who are likely to give you advice on your resumé and interview style (which you don't have to take)

Human resources professionals

• Well-trained interviewers

• Who usually know the company and the boss much better than the agency representative does

• Who have a general idea of the position for which you are interviewing; but

• Who may not know the specifics of the job

Screening interviewers often work from a general job description supplied by the hiring manager, who may want to see only a few applicants. Before passing you on to the hiring manager, the "screener" needs enough information about you to decide whether there is a match between you and the job. The screener is also looking for reasons to screen you out, to eliminate you from further consideration for the position. So, be brief, maintain a positive attitude, and don't volunteer information that could eliminate your candidacy. Negative or superfluous information can make it difficult or impossible to get beyond the screening interview.

Decision interviews
These are often conducted by the prospective supervisor for the open position. Because this is not usually a trained interviewer, he or she may be even more nervous than you are. You can do you both a favor by being at ease, answering all the questions honestly and directly, and asking a few good ones of your own. Help keep the interview going and you'll likely make a good impression.

The boss has three main concerns:

- Can do — do you have the basic skills to handle the job?

- Will do — are you motivated to do the job?

- How fit — will you fit in with the company culture and the other people in your area or department?

Keep these three questions in mind and try to let everything you say reflect positively on what you *can do, will do,* and *how you will fit in.*

If you're asked to attend a second decision interview with the boss's superiors or the department head, don't worry. The decision to hire you may already have been made. The higher-ups just want to formally approve that decision. These decision interviews are often quite brief, and your job qualifications may not be discussed at all. The "big boss" usually just wants to meet you and get a brief impression of how you handle yourself in a business situation. Answer any questions professionally and briefly.

Good research makes for good interviews
Before going to an interview, do enough research on the

company — and, if you can, the position and the interviewer — to make yourself comfortable and knowledgeable. A company is much more than facts, history, products, and a balance sheet. You need to know what it's really like to work there. Is it formal or informal? Relaxed or pressurized? Do people actually talk to each other, or is everything communicated by memo and voice mail?

Before your interview, try to determine:
As much as you can about the company — its history, size, reputation in the industry, major product or service lines, and any major issues facing it today.

Who will be conducting the interview? Is it a screening or decision interview? What is the interviewer's position? Can he or she actually hire you?

Why is this job open? Did the last person to hold it quit after a few months? Or was he or she promoted?

How long has the position been open? Is it hard to fill? Or has the company only recently started looking?

Use your network to research the company and the interviewer. You can also obtain key information from your employment agency if you're using one. The company's own public relations and human resources departments can also provide important data and insights.

When you get to the interview, look around you carefully. Are people chatting in the halls? Are they dressed informally? Or is the atmosphere "strictly business"? Are people introduced as "Ms. Green," "Josephine," or "Jo"? Is there an employee lounge? Is it full or empty?

You may have seen an ad or a job description that includes the skills and other requirements for the job. You need to show your interviewer that your skills and traits are a good match for that position. A good way to do this is to illustrate each trait or skill required with an accomplishment of yours.

Company's criteria
Creative problem-solver

Weak statement	Strong accomplishment statement
"I'm always looking for new ways to solve problems."	"Last summer I came up with a consolidated billing form that eliminated the need for several other forms."

Company's criteria
Excellent communications skills

Weak statement	Strong accomplishment statement
"I communicate well with people."	"In my volunteer position, I was able to attract four new patrons who contributed more than $20,000 to the museum."

It's a good idea to prepare more accomplishment statements than you actually have in your resumé. This assures the interviewer that you have a wide range of desirable skills and traits.

Questions you can ask at on-site interview

Because interviewing is a two-way street, it's a good idea to prepare some of your own questions — thoughtful ones that will communicate your interest and help you learn a lot more about the position and the company. Among the following group of questions, there are probably several you may want to ask at the appropriate time during your interview:

1. Why is this position open?

2. How large is the department, and to whom would I report?

3. Where did the last person in this job go? Why?

4. What are your immediate goals for the person who fills this opening?

5. What are your longer-term objectives for this position?

6. How long do people usually stay in this job?

7. How closely supervised would I be?

8. What equipment would I use? Would I be trained if it were unfamiliar?

9. What are the most difficult or frustrating parts of this position? How can those best be handled?

10. How are people promoted out of this job? Where do they typically go?

11. What changes do you foresee in the department and the company?

12. Do you foresee any staff changes or downsizing in the near future?

13. What kind of person succeeds here?

14. What's the most important skill needed to do this job well?

15. What do you value most in an employee?

16. How do you handle employee problems?

17. How would you describe your management style?

18. How do you characterize the company's culture?

It's best not to ask questions about vacation time, sick leave, or coffee breaks. Doing so might make it seem you're more interested in relaxation than in actually working.

Sample answers to difficult questions

You'll be more confident and relaxed in the interview if you practice good responses to difficult questions. If you're well prepared, you might even be disappointed if the interviewer *doesn't* ask you any "tough" questions. Following is a list of some of the most commonly asked questions — with suggested responses — to help prepare you for almost anything. (Note: some questions may have more than one purpose.)

Interviewer's purpose and questions

Purpose:
Is this person prepared? Organized? Concise?

1. Tell me about yourself.
Answer in about two minutes. Avoid details, don't ramble. Touch on four areas: Where born/raised. Education, military background. Work experience. Current situation.

2. Did you bring your resumé?
Yes. (Be prepared with two or three extra copies.)

3. What do you know about our organization?
Talk about company's products, services, history, and people — especially any friends who work there. "But I would like to know more — particularly from your point of view. Do we have time to cover that now?"

4. According to your definition of success, how successful have you been so far?
Be prepared to define success, then respond.

Purpose:
Is this person mature and self-aware?

5. In your current or last position, what were your most significant accomplishments?
Give one or two accomplishment statements.

6. Would you describe a few situations in which your work was criticized?
Give only one and tell how you have corrected (or plan to correct) the issue.

7. If I spoke with a previous employer, what would he or she say are your greatest strengths and weaknesses?
Be consistent with what you think the employer would say. Position the weakness in a positive way (refer to #10).

8. How would you describe your personality?
Keep your answer short and relevant to the job and the organization's culture.

9. What are your strong points?
Present three. Relate them to the company and the job opening.

10. What are your weak points?
Don't say you have none, but give one that is really a positive in disguise: "I am sometimes impatient and do all the work myself when we are working against tight deadlines."

11. How did you do in school?
Emphasize your best and favorite courses/subject matter. If your GPA was average, talk about your leadership activities or jobs you held to finance your education.

Purpose:
Is this person motivated? What are his/her values, attitudes? Is there a "fit"?

12. What do you look for in a job?
Relate things you enjoy, find challenging in a work environment.

13. How long do you think it would take you to make a meaningful contribution here?
"Not long, I think, because of my experience, my transferable skills, and my ability to learn quickly."

14. How long would you stay with us?
"As long as I feel I'm making a contribution and that my contribution is recognized."

15. If you have never supervised, how do you feel about assuming that responsibility?
Be honest. If you don't want to supervise, emphasize that you can contribute more as an individual player. If you do want to supervise, say so and be enthusiastic.

16. Why do you want to become a supervisor?
"To grow and develop professionally, to help others develop, to build a team, and to share what I have learned."

17. What do you see as the most difficult task in being a supervisor?
"Dealing with different personalities and getting things planned and done through others." If possible, show how you have done this in the past.

18. Describe your ideal working environment.
Refer to a work experiences you have succeeded in. Relate them to this company.

19. Do you prefer working with figures or with words?
Be aware of what the job requires and position your answer (truthfully) in that context.

20. How would your co-workers/fellow students/ professors describe you?
Refer to your strengths and skills.

21. What did you think of your last boss?
If you liked him or her, say so and tell why. If you didn't, find something positive to say.

22. Why do you want to work for a company this size? A company of this type?
Explain how this size or type of company works well for you — using examples from your past if possible.

23. If you had your choice of jobs and companies, where would you go?
Acknowledge that no job is perfect. Say that this job and this company are very close to what best suits you.

24. Why do you want to work for us?

You would like to be part of a company project, to solve a company problem. You like what you've heard about this company, its policies, goals, and management: "I've researched the company and my friends tell me it's a very good place to work."

25. What was the last book you read? Movie you saw? Event you attended?

Think this one through. Your answer should be compatible with the company culture.

26. What kind of hours are you used to working?

"As many hours as it takes to get the job done."
Then ask, "What is an average working day or week here?"

Purpose:
Does this person fit our job and criteria?

27. What would you do for us?

Relate past successes in problem solving that are similar to those of the prospective employer.

28. What has your experience been in supervising people?

Give examples from your accomplishments.

29. How have you helped your previous employers?

Refer to your accomplishments.

30. What is the most money you ever accounted for?

Refer to accomplishments. If you haven't had budget responsibility, say so, but refer to an accomplishment that demonstrates the same skill and responsibility.

31. Describe some situations in which you have worked under pressure or had to meet deadlines.

Refer to accomplishments. Everyone who graduates from college is familiar with pressure and deadlines.

32. Give an example of your creativity.

Refer to accomplishments.

33. Give examples of your leadership abilities.

Draw examples from your accomplishments.

34. What are your career goals?
Talk first about succeeding in the job for which you're applying, then talk about longer-range plans.

35. What position do you expect to have in two years?
"A position similar to the one we're discussing, or the next step up."

36. What are your objectives?
Refer to question #34 on goals. Keep long-range answers fairly general. Short-range, be more specific. Talk about particular skills you want to master, growth opportunities, maybe having more responsibilities or moving into management.

Purpose:
How does this person handle stress?
What is his/her confidence level?

37. Why should we hire you?
Relate a past experience in successful problem solving that may be similar to those of the prospective employer.

38. Why haven't you found a position before now?
"Finding the right job takes time. I'm not looking for just *any* job. And, I think you know what the job market for recent graduates is like today."

39. How much salary do you expect if we offer you this position?
Be careful. If you don't know the market value, return the question by saying you would expect a fair salary based on the job's responsibilities, your experience, skills and education. Ask what salary range has been set for the position. If you know the market value of the job, that may be the key answer, "My understanding is that a job like this one may be in the range of $____. Is that in your ball park?"

Purpose:
What is this person's market value?

40. What kind of salary are you worth?

Ask more about specific responsibilities of the job. This will tell you how important the job is to the company. When the interviewer opens the *real* discussion of salary, you will be in a much better position to determine what the job is worth to both the employer and to you. Delay all mention of money until the end of the interview. If the interviewer insists on a number, quote a range.

41. What other types of jobs or companies are you considering?

"I'm looking at similar positions in several companies." You don't have to be specific.

It may seem awkward at first, but practicing aloud is the best way to rehearse your answers. It's one thing to *think* about what you'll say to a given question, it's quite another to actually say it while observing yourself or *being* observed for feedback. You can practice with someone else, by yourself in front of a mirror, or with an audio tape recorder or video camera.

While reviewing your practice interview, pay attention to:
What you say — the actual meaning you convey.

How you say it — your choice of words, words you omit, and how you "build your case." For instance, "I do best in a flexible environment" is preferable to "I hated the petty rules and regulations at my last job."

Body language and tone of voice — do they support what you're saying or do they contradict your words? If you claim to be energetic and motivated, speak with conviction and sit forward on your chair. It would be hard for an interviewer to believe you if you rarely talked above a whisper and leaned back in your chair during the interview.

What to bring to the interview
Briefcase or folder to hold and protect your papers.

Your resumé — actually bring several extra copies in case the interviewer can't find his or her copy. You'll also want to have one to refer to, yourself.

Your own data sheet to help you complete the employment application quickly.

A notebook, appointment calendar, and a pen to jot down important information or to schedule your next interview with the company. (Don't take extensive notes during the interview, however. This precludes good eye contact and will distract your attention from what is being said.)

Weather-related accessories. If you forget your umbrella and are caught in a downpour you won't look very professional.

Be early

The only way to make sure you'll be on time is to allow plenty of extra time for exigencies. Remember Murphy's Law: "Whatever can go wrong will go wrong." If nothing does, you'll be early — allowing you time to catch your breath, read over your resumé at a relaxed pace, and to introduce yourself to the secretary or receptionist. Being early also gives you a moment to check your appearance in a mirror and tend to any grooming needs that will make you feel more self-confident.

Take time to be friendly. Get the receptionist's or secretary's name and make some light conversation. Practice projecting confidence when you speak. Even though this person may not have a lot of influence with the boss (though you shouldn't assume this), you'll be able to hear your own voice. This can help relax you.

If you have a coat, umbrella, or other bulky items, ask if you can leave them out front with the receptionist so you won't be burdened when you meet the interviewer. Pay attention to your breathing during the time you're waiting. Deep breaths will make you feel more relaxed. Waiting also gives you the opportunity to survey the office environment. Get a feeling of what kind of place it is. You may be able to overhear office conversations (but don't appear to be actively listening). All these cues and clues can help you assess the office atmosphere.

Make a good first impression

During the first few seconds of an interview, while you are still meeting the interviewer and getting seated and ready to go, you'll be conveying some impressions which often lead the interviewer subconsciously to reach a conclusion about you. It's far easier to build on this first impression than to turn it around. That's why a good, positive first impression is so important.

Dress to your advantage in a style that's consistent with the type of position for which you are applying. Conservative dress is always appropriate. Of course, there could be jobs where a more flamboyant style would fit perfectly. In northern and metropolitan areas, dark conservative attire is usually safest. In more rural areas, less formal — even sporty clothing — may be appropriate. Check into the style of dress in this new work community, particularly for the organization where you're interviewing.

The objective is to "fit the environment" where you'd like to work. Naturally, you'll want to be sure your shoes are polished and your hair and nails are well groomed. Jewelry should be sparse. Women's makeup should be appropriate for business.

Interview rooms tend to be small, so go easy on the perfume or after-shave. A deodorant or antiperspirant is a wise bet for this "nervous" occasion. And, if you're having a meal before the interview, skip the garlic, spicy foods, and alcohol.

If you're a smoker, forget it. Smoking today is "verboten" in most office environments. And gum chewing just isn't appropriate to the situation. If you must, smoke or chew outside the building — before you introduce yourself to the receptionist.

Being well prepared for your interview lets you focus your attention on the interview and the interviewer. If you aren't distracted and if you haven't forgotten something, you'll be far better able to concentrate on the matter at hand. Pleasing the customer is the goal of all marketing efforts. This is your marketing effort for *you*. And you'll need to pay full attention to your "customer," the interviewer. Getting off to a good start is essential. And you only have this one chance to do this right.

A firm handshake, a genuine smile, and good eye contact go a long way toward creating a positive first impression. Wait for the interviewer to sit down or offer you a chair before taking a seat yourself. If you're not sure where to sit, ask.

The dialogue

There's no need to blurt out your best and most significant attributes the minute you sit down. Let the conversation develop naturally. It will likely take you and the interviewer a few minutes to become comfortable with each other, to establish some rapport, and to bring your concentration to the matter at hand. A little small talk is appropriate — the weather, last night's big ball score — whatever is appropriate. But it's best to let the interviewer initiate the small talk. Try to get the interviewer to talk about himself early. This will give you a better idea of his interests and style of communicating. But, don't be pushy. Let the interviewer control the conversation. And never interrupt in your eagerness to get a point across.

I-SPEAK Your Language®

The I-SPEAK communication styles concept provides clues to help you identify the speaking (and thinking) style of other people, and ways to interact appropriately with each style.

I-SPEAK Your Language, a proprietary program of Drake Beam Morin, Inc., is based on extensive research done by Dr. Carl Jung, the noted Swiss psychologist. Jung's studies reveal that everyone has four styles of communication available, but one style tends to dominate. Familiarity with the four styles allows you to recognize your own and other people's styles. And this familiarity will give you a quick sense of how to communicate with others most effectively.

I-SPEAK is based on four premises:

1. All individuals have recognizable communication styles;

2. It is possible to identify an individual's style after a relatively brief exposure to it;

3. People communicate most effectively with styles that are similar to their own; and,

4. People can adapt or modify their styles to "speak the language" of others.

DBM has adapted this theory to help you characterize your own and others' primary and back-up communication styles. No style is considered good or bad; no style is preferred or considered more "right" than another.

Style	Communication focus
Intuitor	Conceiving, projecting, inducing
Thinker	Analyzing, ordering thoughts in a logical fashion
Feeler	Understanding experience through emotional reactions and response to feelings
Senser	Taking action mainly on the basis of one's own sensory perceptions

Intuitor style

Intuitors are individuals who place emphasis on ideas, innovation, and long-range thinking. They reveal an imagination, but can be viewed as "hard to pin down and understand." At times, Intuitors can be seen as "long on vision, but short on action." Intuitors are typically less interested in what has been done before than what should be done in the future. The Intuitor values communications that are well thought out and direct and that do not waste time or space on details.

Thinker style

Thinkers respond well to logic, new ideas, and systematic inquiry. They function in a steady, tenacious manner, and are often quite skeptical of their own and others' initial reactions and formulations. They are less concerned with making the so-called dramatic breakthrough than in correctly and consistently relating a present course of action to both the past and the future. Thinkers value communications that are well organized, systematic and logical. They emphasize facts, well-documented conclusions, and specifics. When possible, they will omit adjectives, judgments, and feelings unless they are necessary to the facts.

Feeler style

Feelers focus on human interaction. They seek and enjoy the stimulation of contact with others and express concern for people and an understanding of them. They are usually quite astute in "reading between the lines." They relate human experiences to the context of the past. As Feelers grow older, they may become sentimental and they value communications that sound personal rather than impersonal or cold. They rely on illustrations based on real people in real situations.

Senser style

Sensers focus on action; they see the specific actions of others as a better indication of their commitments than any other responses. They will engage in activities that provide them with the opportunity for tangible and immediate feedback. They are frequently viewed as the driving force within an organization, and are sought out for their energy and ability to translate ideas into products, sales and profits. Sensers appreciate a specific and pragmatic approach. They are action-oriented — they want to know what others intend to do; what is expected of themselves; why; in what way; and for what purpose.

You will benefit from being familiar with all four I-SPEAK styles, as well as from an understanding of the style or styles most comfortable for you. In your job search communications, try to assess and adapt to the style of the person with whom you're talking. Knowledge of the I-SPEAK styles, together with well-honed active listening skills, can greatly enhance your communications capabilities in an interview.

(Note: Drake Beam Morin offers a full line of I-SPEAK Your Language products in English and Spanish which can help you more readily identify and respond appropriately to the four I-SPEAK styles. For more information, contact DBM toll-free at 800-345-JOBS.)

The heart of the interview

You have a limited amount of time to "make the sale" in an interview. Remember your objective: convince the customer — through an honest and positive presentation and by establishing good rapport — that you are the best candidate for the job. And use your time wisely.

You will come across as a strong candidate if you answer questions positively and succinctly, relating your skills and experience to job requirements. Get as much information about the position as you can early in the interview. Using this information, you can highlight your related experiences and avoid volunteering information that is not relevant. By providing brief and informative answers, you allow the interviewer to steer the discussion, asking about the things that most interest him or her.

Be sure you understand a question before attempting to answer it. You want to address the interviewer's particular concerns. If the question is not clear, ask for clarification rather than guessing what is meant. This simple approach can prevent your getting off on the wrong track. Also, in answering briefly, it's fine to ask if you have answered the question sufficiently or whether the interviewer would like more detail. This question allows you to use your time wisely and to address only those issues of importance to the interviewer. As with all interview techniques, don't overuse either of these approaches. Use your own good judgment in both presenting information and requesting or offering clarification.

Relating your ability and experience to the job in question is the strongest sales argument there is. Relate your actual accomplishments proudly and you will be less likely to find yourself bragging or claiming you can do anything. Sticking to the relevant facts will make both you and the interviewer more comfortable.

You'll also come across well by presenting information in a positive light and avoiding negatives. It's especially important to be positive — as well as brief — in discussing your reasons for seeking work in a particular geographic area and your past work experiences including part-time and summer jobs while in school. Talk in terms of "challenges" rather than "problems." Briefly describe what job-related opportunities the job offers you. And avoid, at all costs, any long story portraying the horrors of past employers or positions. Religion and politics are two more inappropriate and dangerous topics. Name-dropping is considered politics. Unless you met the interviewer through a mutual acquaintance within the company, it's best not to mention the other person's name. It could work against you as well as in your favor.

Salary can be controversial. If you can delay a discussion of money until the end of the interview, do so. If you're asked early on about your minimum requirement, try to counter with your "need to learn more about the scope of the job." Your negotiating position will be stronger after you've sold the interviewer that you're the person the company needs. However, don't let the issue of whether to discuss salary become a point of controversy. Be prepared to state the range of your salary expectations at any point in the interview. This range should be based on comparative data for this type of position, at your level of experience, within this industry.

Interviews can be more enjoyable and productive for both you and the person across the desk if you can sustain a meaningful dialogue. Continue to ask appropriate questions during the heart of the interview. Learn about the interviewer's views. And watch for opportunities to ask questions that demonstrate that you've done some research on the company.

Monitor the tone of the discussion. If it should become negative, try to change it. Ask a tactful question or try to introduce another relevant topic. This is not the time for being either critical or argumentative. The interviewer, remember, is your "customer." And you know what they say about "customers"!

Ending the interview

Try to end the interview on a positive note. If the dialogue has been enjoyable, say so. If your discussion has made you enthusiastic about the position, let the interviewer know. Genuine enthusiasm may help you win the interview...and the job. Everyone wants to work with people who are both qualified and positive.

At the end of most interviews, many interviewers will ask if you have any further questions. If you do, ask them. If you don't, express your appreciation for the interviewer's time and express your genuine interest in the position you've been discussing. Then, you might add something like, "I'm very interested in this position. Could you give me a general idea of how my qualifications and background fit with your concept of the 'ideal candidate'?" A question like this is far better than, "Well, what do you think? How did I do?"

Before you leave, make sure you understand the next steps. If no specific arrangement has been established to contact you, ask when they expect to make some preliminary evaluation. Then propose a date for contacting the interviewer. There is no need to be defensive about this. Interviewers sometimes simply forget to tie up the loose ends. And you're demonstrating follow-through, which is a good business practice.

Interviewing do's and don'ts

- Don't ramble

- Stop talking when you have answered the question

- After you're asked a question, take a moment before you answer

- Be sure you hear the question, then respond to it directly

- Use positive terms

- Maintain good eye contact with your interviewer and smile appropriately

- Seize opportunities to point out how you could help your new employer

- Avoid sounding mechanical in your answers; sound thoughtful

- Don't "overanswer" — giving too much information can be worse than too little

- The corollary to this is simply, "be brief"

- Don't promise too much

- Don't argue with the interviewer

- Don't let the interviewer ask all the questions; take part in a dialogue

- Don't let a few moments of silence make you say the wrong thing

- Be honest in your answers

- Try to relax

The follow-up letter
Within 48 hours after an interview, it's good form to send a cordial follow-up letter to the person with whom you spoke. This letter should:

Thank the person for the interview

Emphasize your interest in the position under consideration

Re-phrase your background and briefly explain how your experience can complement the requirements of the position

State anything you wish you had made clearer — or forgot to mention — in the interview

Indicate that you look forward to hearing his or her decision (refer to the follow-up agreed to) or say that you will follow up to determine if and when the interviewer wants to see you again.

Another way of recalling the construction of this follow-up letter is "The 4 Rs":

Remember — As most people don't take the time to send follow-up letters, yours will stand out and help the interviewer remember you.

Reinforce — In a sentence or two, restate the skills, accomplishments, and experience that make you right for this job.

Recoup — If there's something you wish you had made clearer — or forgot to say in the interview — you can state it now in your letter.

Remind — In the closing paragraph, you can tactfully remind the interviewer of a promise or agreement. ("Thank you for your interest and encouragement. I look forward to hearing from you by next Wednesday to learn the date of my next interview.")

Here's a sample "follow-up" letter:

Barbara Gardner
1234 54 Street
New York, NY 10017
June 24, 1993

Ms. Alice Mann
Employment Director
ABC Hotels, Inc.
123 Main Street
Rochester, NY 11111

Dear Ms. Mann:

(Remember) I appreciated the opportunity to meet with you yesterday to learn more about your organization. It was also thoughtful of you to introduce me to Gail Graf and John Slingerland.

(Reinforce) As we discussed, my education in hotel/motel management at Cornell and my three years' experience with Hyatt Hotels would indicate a good fit for the position as Banquet Director. The position would make good use of my detail-orientation, planning abilities, and experience handling major corporate customers.

(Recoup) When we discussed my computer skills, I'm not sure I made it clear that I'll be concluding my training on Lotus 1-2-3 next week. I'm sure this could be helpful during budget reviews.

(Remind) I have a strong interest in the position, and I will phone you next Tuesday as you suggested.

Sincerely,

Barbara Gardner

Negotiating the job offer

What is negotiable?

Many recent graduates seeking their first career position don't believe they're in a position to negotiate anything. A common attitude seems to be, "Negotiating is only for top people, especially in a tight job market; people at our level take what's offered." However, that just isn't the case — even today. Though the salary may be a "given" (and many times, it isn't), there are other aspects of a job that can be negotiated.

Negotiation is not simply bargaining about salary; it is the process through which you and the employer agree on the terms of your employment. These terms can be broken down into four parts:

The job — its title or level, responsibilities, location, any duties for supervising others or managing projects, reporting relationships, and opportunities for advancement.

Conditions of employment — your start date, work schedule, travel requirements, and opportunities for "flex time."

Benefits — such as vacation time, sick pay, health and life insurance, corporate-paid child care, tuition reimbursement, and much more.

Salary — including your starting salary, the frequency of salary reviews, and any bonuses.

Here's a list of things that can often be negotiated:

Compensation:
Base salary
Overtime
Sales commissions
Bonuses
Money in place of benefits

Benefits:
"Cafeteria" benefit plan
Personal days off
Extra vacation time *
Insurance programs:
Medical
Dental
Life
Long-term disability
Financial programs:
Stock options *
Corporate performance
Participation plan
Company-paid pension
/annuity
Matching investment
/profit-sharing programs *
401K plan
Thrift plan
Educational programs:
Tuition reimbursement
Education/training expenses
Professional association memberships

Perquisites:
Flexible schedule ("flex time")
Expense account
Carfare reimbursement
Liberal gas allowance
Free lunches
Company-paid (or sponsored)
child care

Severance provisions:
Outplacement services
Severance settlement

Employee services:
Annual physical exam
Legal, tax, financial assistance
Loans and mortgages at reduced
rates

Discounts on purchases:
Computer equipment
Word processing
Free company services (free
checking from a bank, etc.)
On-premises health club

* = often offered only to executives

Because you are negotiating for a "mix" of these items, you should know what is most important to you. Do not assume just because you are an entry-level employee that a seemingly "executive" benefit is not available to you; explore all options, tactfully, of course.

You might want to go over this list of negotiable items and mark each one with an A, B, or C. Those you mark "A" are essential — you truly believe you must have these. "B" items are important, but not essential. And, "C" items are less important and can be traded for other items that are more important. However, keep your "A" list short if you haven't had much full-time work experience. Don't end up sounding presumptuous or foolish by coming in with a laundry list of demands. Determine items that are likely negotiable by asking the advice of a company "insider" or a career counselor.

What must you have? You may require a minimum salary level or carfare allowance. If these requirements are not part of the offer, you should be prepared to turn the position down or go back to the drawing board and review what you truly must have. (In addition to your minimum acceptable salary, you should also have a desired salary in mind.)

What is *important?* Health or some other type of insurance? These items are desirable, but not essential. You may be prepared to be flexible on one of these items to get one of your "must have" items.

What is *less important?* A full week's vacation? A higher sales commission? You can easily be flexible on — or even give up — one of these items in exchange for a higher priority item.

Know what the employer is willing to offer
Use your networking contacts to get a good idea of the salary range for entry-level positions such as the one you're seeking — within your industry and, if possible, within the company you're interviewing. Does the company have a "grade system"? What grades apply to this job and

what are the high and low salaries for each grade? How flexible is the company (and the boss) on other important items such as flex time, commuting allowances, personal leave, and overtime?

If you can't learn this information through networking, you can ask these questions at some point during a subsequent interview. Negotiations begin *only* after a firm job offer is made by the employer. Don't try to start negotiating before you have the offer. In fact, before the offer, it's usually a good idea not to mention salary at all. Instead, wait for the interviewer to bring it up.

Here are some guidelines for negotiating:

Decision interviews
Informal negotiations usually begin here as the employer sizes-up what you can contribute to the organization and you estimate your worth to this employer. It is still too early to begin formal negotiations because the employer is not sure that he wants to extend an offer, and the job may not yet have been fully defined. You can't arrive at a compensation level when you don't know the exact job responsibilities or the company's established performance standards.

If you have had a comparable full-time position recently and the interviewer asks what you are making — or if you're asked what your expected salary is at this early stage — you might say, "Could we get back to that after I learn more about responsibilities of the position?" If the interviewer persists, you can respond with, "I know the salary range at some other companies, but I don't know yours. What is the range for this position?" Whatever you do at this stage, avoid quoting an actual figure.

If the number is too high, you may price yourself out of the market. If the figure is too low, the employer will know he doesn't have to offer you a nickel more. Some interviewers, hearing a low-ball figure, may think the candidate is under-qualified for the position. So, ask for a range. And, if you're pressed, respond with a range yourself. The figure you're trying to get to should be somewhere in the middle of the range. For example, if you're looking for $25,000, you might say you're looking at positions in the $22,000 to $27,500 range.

Try to get the interviewer to show his or her cards first. Negotiating is a lot like poker: the player who shows his cards first is at a disadvantage. That's why you ask the interviewer for a range before giving one yourself. During the decision interview stage, you can strengthen your negotiating position by concentrating on *building value* and *looking for signals of an offer.*

Building value
When you enter an interview room, your value to the potential employer hasn't yet been established. Throughout the interview, you can build that value by discussing your accomplishments —particularly those that apply to your potential employer's situation. Later, when it's time to make an offer, the employer will be more likely to be flexible on compensation or terms of employment in order to hire a valuable addition to the staff. If you've never had a full-time job, choose accomplishments from academic life or part-time jobs that indicate you have skills valuable to the employer. These might include organizational skills and demonstrated leadership ability.

Reading the signals of an offer
There are definite signals that indicate you have established your value to the company, and that the firm is now seriously considering making you an offer. Some of these include:

• The interview runs longer than planned

• You are asked back for a second or third interview

• The interviewer tries to "sell" you on the company

• The interviewer is very specific about salary, benefits, and/or start date

• The interviewer says he or she will call your references soon

- The interviewer wants you to meet his or her boss or someone else of higher authority

Negotiating the job offer

When you receive an offer, don't respond immediately. The position won't evaporate if you ask for a day or two to think the offer over. Employers know that some new grads may have several offers, and most will give you some "decision time." Thank the interviewer or whomever makes you the offer, then ask for a meeting to discuss it further. As you go over each part of the package you've been offered, use your list of "A," "B," and "C" items to determine how you really feel about it and how it fits with your true needs.

If a job offer meets your expectations, your decision should be fairly easy. However, if the offer is borderline, you may need to ask yourself some questions:

Are my original guidelines realistic or should I modify them?

Have I really used up all my good leads...and is this the best offer I'm likely to get?

How long would it take to find new job leads? Good ones?

How is my money and my patience holding out? Should I take this job and start looking for a better one when I've gained some experience and am financially more stable?

Remember that negotiating is not arguing! Ask to review and discuss all parts of the offer with the person who made it — with the intent of arriving at an agreement that is satisfactory to you both. You may wind up working for this person, and if you negotiate too aggressively, it may affect that working relationship. Always remain calm, friendly, and flexible. If an employer says an item is not negotiable, go on to one which is.

Accepting or rejecting an offer

When you receive a verbal offer you want to accept, it's a good idea to:

Find out if there are other conditions to meet before you are employed — such as a medical exam or further reference checks.

Discuss your understanding of the employment agreement with your boss to make sure major points are mutually understood.

Ask for a written offer that contains the major points you have agreed on. If this is not the company's policy, write your own letter to the company (to your superior) which outlines the agreement and your acceptance of the job. Keep a copy of this letter in case there are any misunderstandings later on.

If you decide to reject an offer, *don't burn your bridges.* This is especially true if you've spent a lot of time negotiating with the company. Phone the person who extended the offer, explain why you are declining, and follow up with a brief note of appreciation. (It is well to remember that you may wind up working for this company later in your career.) If you are rejecting an offer because the salary is too low, there's a chance the company may get back to you with a better figure or package. Keep your options open, though, and continue your job search until you actually begin your new job.

Cost of living comparisons

In starting their careers, many recent graduates move to a new city — either by choice or because the job happens to be there. But, it's important to remember that the buying power of a given income depends to a large degree on where you live. This makes it prudent to consider a city's cost of living in order to determine whether a given salary will actually meet your needs.

Average City, USA = 100.0

To compare two cities, use the index number for each city and plug them into this equation: [10]

$$\frac{(City\ \#1)}{(City\ \#2)} \quad \frac{Index\ \#\ times\ salary}{Index\ \#} \quad = \$$$

How much does a person in Atlanta need to earn annually to have the buying power of someone making $25,000 a year in San Diego?

$$\frac{Atlanta}{San\ Diego} \quad \frac{98.8\ x\ \$25,000}{132.3} \quad = \$18,670$$

How much does a person in San Diego need to earn annually to have the buying power of someone making $25,000 a year in Atlanta?

$$\frac{San\ Diego}{Atlanta} \quad \frac{132.3\ x\ \$25,000}{98.8} \quad = \$33,477$$

10. *National Business Employment Weekly*, Special Spring/Summer 1993 Edition, page 35.

Cost of living index by state and major city

Alabama

Birmingham	101.5
Huntsville	97.0

Alaska

Anchorage	131.7

Arizona

Phoenix	98.7
Tucson	106.5

Arkansas

Fayetteville	90.2
Fort Smith	89.1

California

Bakersfield	115.8
Los Angeles	130.1
Palm Springs	120.8
San Diego	132.3

Colorado

Boulder	105.9
Colorado Springs	94.0
Denver	103.0

Connecticut

Hamden	130.2

Delaware

Wilmington	112.5

Washington DC 134.7

Florida

Jacksonville	95.3
Miami	106.5
Orlando	98.9
Tampa	95.6
West Palm	110.1

Georgia
Atlanta   98.8

Idaho
Boise   103.7

Illinois
Bloomington   104.1
Champaign   100.7
Peoria   104.2

Indiana
Indianapolis   95.3
South Bend   92.7

Iowa
Des Moines   102.3

Kansas
Lawrence   94.7

Kentucky
Lexington   99.2
Louisville   91.8

Louisiana
Baton Rouge   99.0
New Orleans   96.8

Maryland
Hagerstown   97.9

Massachusetts
Boston   136.9

Michigan
Benton Harbor   102.8
Lansing   101.4

Minnesota
Minneapolis   100.2
St. Paul   106.7

Missouri

Kansas City	95.5
St. Louis	96.6

Montana

Billings	104.9

Nebraska

Lincoln	89.2
Omaha	91.1

Nevada

Las Vegas	109.3
Reno/Sparks	109.6

New Hampshire

Manchester	113.7

New Mexico

Albuquerque	99.3
Santa Fe	108.7

New York

Albany	112.4
Binghamton	99.1
New York City	214.2
Syracuse	101.1

North Carolina

Charlotte	99.6
Raleigh/Durham	97.7
Winston-Salem	96.1

North Dakota

Minot	95.1

Ohio

Cincinnati	103.5
Cleveland	110.1
Columbus	107.6

Oklahoma

Oklahoma City	91.1
Tulsa	88.3

Oregon
Portland   108.2
Salem   100.0

Pennsylvania
Allentown   108.7
Harrisburg   104.3
Lancaster   109.6
Philadelphia   131.5

South Carolina
Charleston   99.8

South Dakota
Sioux Falls   93.4

Tennessee
Knoxville   94.9
Memphis   94.2
Nashville   92.2

Texas
Amarillo   86.4
Dallas   103.8
El Paso   97.9
Fort Worth   94.5
Houston   99.0
Lubbock   92.2
San Antonio   92.7

Utah
Provo/Orem   99.1
Salt Lake City   96.2

Vermont
Montpelier   109.6

Virginia
Prince William   115.2
Richmond   105.2
Roanoke   93.4

Washington

Seattle	117.7
Spokane	102.5

West Virginia

Charleston	101.7
Berkeley County	92.4

Wisconsin

Eau Claire	95.6
Green Bay	96.8
La Crosse	98.7
Milwaukee	104.9

Wyoming

Cheyenne	96.6

Source: American Chamber of Commerce Researchers Association Inter-City Cost of Living Index, Third Quarter 1992.

Note: This index, produced by the American Chamber of Commerce Researchers Association, is updated quarterly and reflects the cost of housing, transportation, health care and various consumer items, but excludes taxes. Cities listed here are those with chambers of commerce which volunteered to participate in the survey. Major cities not listed had chambers which did not participate.

After you're hired:
Survival strategies
on your new job

Congratulations! You've worked hard and you've won your first real career position — the job of your choice. Now you will want to take a few minutes to think about *succeeding* in that job and preparing...yes, beginning even now...for your next position. Because what you do in and *with* this job — beginning your first day — will determine to an unexpected degree what and *where* that next job will be.

First, the housekeeping matters
At the close of your final meeting prior to actually starting your new job, make sure you get the following information:

The job's location, work hours, and the name of your immediate superior

What employment papers you need to complete — sometimes these can be filled out before you actually report for work

Whether the company typically announces new employees' names, positions, and backgrounds — perhaps in a newsletter or press release. If so, ask if your employment can be so announced

If the company or organization has an employee hand-book, try to obtain a copy so that you can read it over before actually starting to work

Be sure you are at least on time — early is better — the first day on the job. Ask your boss or a co-worker what the customs and practices are concerning any break times, lunch time, and when the day ends for your group or department. And, dress the part of a professional person reporting for a new position. Sometimes today the dress code can be pretty relaxed in some organizations. Find out what is appropriate. If it seems your wardrobe isn't quite up to the culture of your new company, it might be wise to invest in some new clothes. And, by the way, that *is* what you'll be doing — investing in yourself and in your future. The whole idea is to look, act, and conduct yourself as would the person you seek to become. Do that consistently and you will *become* that person.

Try to learn what became of the person who held your position before you were hired. Was he or she promoted? Terminated? Did the person quit? The fate of your prede-cessor isn't necessarily tied to your own in any way. (Unless the job is impossible to do and no amount of effort will result in success — which probably isn't true for most entry-level jobs.) You may have heard something about your predecessor during your interviews. However, after you've been employed for awhile, you might ask a friendly peer. Sometimes the truth isn't exactly what the company puts out for public consumption.

Getting off to the right start with your boss
Your relationship with your immediate superior is the most important relationship you're going to encounter. What is your boss's communication style? How does he or she think and consistently express himself? Check back to "I-SPEAK" personality types in the chapter on interviewing. What is your boss? A feeler, thinker, senser or intuitor? Identifying the communication style can go a long way to helping you communicate more clearly, precisely, and convincingly with your superior. Another

thing: some people prefer to have things in writing that they can read; others prefer to *hear* the same types of things verbally. Try to determine which type your boss is. This will give you important insight into how you should present — ideas, issues, questions, and problems — more effectively to this person.

It is an excellent idea to ask for a brief meeting with your immediate superior early on to make certain you are in alignment on your job responsibilities, duties, and priorities. You should have a reasonably good idea of these based on your interviews. Sometimes it makes sense for you and your boss both to fill out a list of the five most important things for you to concentrate on doing. When you compare your lists, at least three of the items should be the same. If they aren't, ask for guidance and direction.

Ascertain what your group's practice is concerning performance reviews. These regular sessions with your boss help you understand how your activities and results compare with his or her expectations. In many companies, performance reviews are held semi-annually. During your first six months or so, you might suggest an informal meeting every two or three months until you have begun to "settle in" to the new job. And, you might mark your calendar so that you can remind the boss — in writing — a day or two before the appointed date. During the performance review, you will want to discuss what has gone well, any problems you've encountered, and how you've resolved them. You should expect the boss's honest appraisal of your work and recommendations for improvement. If you don't get these, tactfully ask for them.

Relationships
Getting along with co-workers — at all levels — is essential. Not only is it essential to your success in your position and in your career, but you'll find good working relationships increasingly important to your happiness on the job and your satisfaction as an employee. Being friendly, helpful, cooperative, and willing to "dig in" and do your share are all traits that will win high marks among those with whom you'll be working.

Be careful about office politics; they can be deadly. Until you truly know the territory, it's best to avoid joining any "cliques or cabals." You might also be justifiably wary of any one person who seems to seek you out with great vigor. There may be some ulterior motive at work there. You can hardly go wrong if you're cordial and friendly with everyone.

It's fine to be sociable, too. Lunch dates with colleagues, dinner parties at someone's home, working together on charitable or professional projects are all excellent means for getting to know your associates and your organization better. And, while norms do vary about "togetherness" in companies, social occasions provide the opportunity to gain a lot of useful information and to get the kind of "right" exposure that can forward your career.

Avoid overtly competitive behaviors toward other people. In college, you were on your own most of the time. In this environment, people get work done by working together — in concert if not actually in tandem. The "team player" may be a cliché, but such a person is still highly valued. You will further your own career if you can become a good one.

Learn where the power lies. Sometimes it's not where an outsider would think it is. The secretary who is the real power behind her boss is more typical than you might believe. Before you *know* who has the power, be wary of crossing anyone. *After* you know, it's still best not to cross anyone.

A final word
Two words, actually: *have fun!* You've come a long way since graduation. You've put a lot of time and effort into securing the position that will launch your career. There's a lot riding on this job. So put everything you've got into doing it to the very best of your ability; no one can ask for more. And, remember, too — there's a great "ride" ahead.

There's just no *telling* where or how high you can go in your career. The sky truly is the limit for enthusiastic, well educated, highly motivated and skilled young people in the workplace of the '90s and beyond.

You've got a great life ahead. Enjoy it!

Bibliography

Adams, Bob. *The Complete Resumé & Job Search Book for College Students*. Holbrook, MA: Bob Adams, Inc., 1992.

Drake, John D., Ph.D. *The Campus Interview*. New York: Drake Beam Morin, Inc., 1981.

DBM Publishing. *Managing Stress in Turbulent Times*. New York, 1993.

DBM Publishing. *Seven Imperatives for Fair, Legal and Productive Interviewing*. New York, 1993.

Fein, Richard. *First Job: A new grad's guide to launching your business career*. New York: John Wiley & Sons, Inc., 1992.

Fox, Marcia R. *Put Your Degree to Work: The new professional's guide to career planning and job hunting*. New York: W. W. Norton & Company, 1988.

Lindquist, Victor R. *The Northwestern Lindquist-Endicott Report 1993*. Evanston, IL: The Placement Center of Northwestern University, 1992.

Morin, William J., and James C. Cabrera. *Parting Company: How to survive the loss of a job and find another successfully*. San Diego, CA: Harcourt Brace Jovanovich, 1991.

Pedersen, Laura. *Street-smart Career Guide: A step-by-step program for your career development.* New York: Crown Publishers, Inc., 1993.

Rogers, Edward J. *Getting Hired: Everything you need to know about resumés, interviews, and job-hunting strategies.* New York: Prentice Hall Press, 1982.

Tener, Elizabeth. *The Smith College Job Guide.* New York: Penguin Books USA, Inc., 1991.

About Drake Beam Morin, Inc.

Drake Beam Morin, Inc. (DBM) is the world's leading human resources management consulting firm. DBM provides organizations and their employees with the highest caliber services and products available in the areas of employee selection, performance and transition management.

Since 1967, we have assisted more than 50,000 organizations of all types and sizes and over one million individuals at all employee levels. This wealth of experience, which far surpasses any other firm in the industry, enables DBM to offer organizations the expertise that most effectively and efficiently meets their human resources challenges.

Through a network of over 150 locations around the globe, DBM provides personalized attention on a local level, along with a vast array of resources, wherever you may be located. With DBM, you have the best of two worlds: a local firm with global presence.

To find out more about how any of DBM's programs can benefit your organization, contact your local DBM office or DBM Corporate Headquarters, 100 Park Avenue, New York, NY 10017, 212 692-7700.